M000014442

Presented to

_____

by

_____

On the Occasion of

_____

Date

_____

I GIVE MYSELF TO PRAYER

*Devotional Thoughts
on Prayers from the Psalms*

DANIEL PARTNER

BARBOUR BOOKS
An Imprint of Barbour Publishing, Inc.

Published by Barbour Books, an imprint of Barbour Publishing, Inc., P.O. Box 719, Uhrichsville, Ohio 44683
http://www.barbourbooks.com

 Member of the
Evangelical Christian
Publishers Association

Printed in the United States of America.

I GIVE MYSELF
TO PRAYER

In memory of my father,
Dan Partner,
who came to Christ late in life
and died too soon.

INTRODUCTION

The Greeks called them "psalms" (songs). The Hebrews named them *Tehillim* (praises or songs of praise). Christians call this biblical collection of 150 hymns and poems the "Psalter." These are hymns of praise acclaiming God as creator of the world, ruler of history, and king of Jerusalem; they are prayers and laments recited in times of personal crisis and in times of national peril and woe; they are songs of faith and trust in God; they are wisdom, teaching, meditation, accusation, and rebuke.

These are the Psalms.

Seventy-four are attributed to the Hebrew king David. Twelve are believed to have been written by his son Solomon. Moses wrote one psalm and other poets wrote thirty-two. The remainder are anonymous.

All in all, the book of Psalms is an astonishing anthology of ancient spiritual verse. Jesus Christ himself quoted the Psalms, and it is likely that the first Christians sang some of them when they gathered. In the fifth century,

Augustine called the book of Psalms the "language of devotion," and a thousand years later Martin Luther called it "a Bible in miniature."

The little book you hold in your hand is a collection of seventy-five prayers drawn from the wondrous book of Psalms. Sacred meanings contained in each prayer are amplified by a short thought or meditation freshly composed for this book.

I have gathered these prayers and thoughts together in hope that they will enrich you with God's Spirit and with truth as you pray and sing and make melody in your heart to the Lord, giving thanks to God the Father for everything in the name of our Lord Jesus Christ (Ephesians 5:18–20).

DANIEL PARTNER
Sisters, Oregon
January 2002

FOR *my love they are my adversaries: But I give myself unto prayer.*

PSALM 109:4

LORD,

how are they increased that trouble me!
many are they that rise up against me.
Many there be which say of my soul,
There is no help for him in God.
But thou, O LORD, art a shield for me;
my glory, and the lifter up of mine head.
I cried unto the LORD with my voice,
and he heard me out of his holy hill.
I laid me down and slept;
I awaked; for the LORD sustained me.

PSALM 3:1–5

THIS
PRAYER
WAS PRAYED

by a man who was being hunted down by his own son. The Old Testament book of 2 Samuel tells how Absalom rebelled against his father David, the king of Israel, and attempted to kill him and seize the throne. Ancient historians told this tangled story through seven biblical chapters (13–19). But David recounts the experience in these few simple lines of poetry. And here, as in all of David's psalms, he does not even mention the name of his son.

But David had certainly not forgotten Absalom. Ask any parent who has endured the rebellion of a child—we mourn for them just as David did: "O my son Absalom! My son, my son Absalom! If only I could have died instead of you! O Absalom, my son, my son" (2 Samuel 18:33 NLT).

Though David was a gifted writer, he left it to others to recount the tragedy of Absalom. Instead, he told God of troubles so extreme that people said there was even "no help for him in God."

Could there be no help for us in the

world? This is likely. No help in family or friends? This could be. But no help in God? Impossible. So David declared the power of God, "Thou, O LORD, art a shield for me; my glory, and the lifter up of mine head." And then he prayed, crying to the Lord with his voice.

"And [God] heard me out of his holy hill." David was in hiding far away from God's holy hill in Jerusalem. How did he know God had heard his prayer? David's faith assured him of this. And his faith was the same as yours: the confident assurance that what you hope for has happened or will happen (see Hebrews 11:1). And what a hope—that God would hear your voice in prayer!

In testimony of this, David tells of how soundly he could sleep, despite his troubles: "I laid me down and slept; I awaked; for the LORD sustained me." David made his requests known to God and his heart and mind was kept by "the peace of God, which passeth all understanding" (Philippians 4:6–7).

HEAR

me when I call,
O God of my righteousness:
thou hast enlarged me when I was in distress;
have mercy upon me, and hear my prayer.

PSALM 4:1

WHEN I WAS A LITTLE BOY,

an alley connected the backyard of my house with the garage of our neighbor Mr. Hanlan. There he kept a treasury of tools. Sometimes my dad would send me to ask Mr. Hanlan for some tool that was not in his own collection. So I'd trot the half block down the alley, enter our neighbor's garage through a beat-up door, and ask for the tool.

Mr. Hanlan probably wouldn't have given me any tools for my own use. But he knew I wasn't asking for myself. My requests for tools were made in my dad's name. That's why Mr. Hanlan would entrust me with the tool.

This explains why people end their prayers with the saying, "In the name of Jesus." We cannot effectively pray in our own names, because we have no righteousness. Mr. Hanlan had no reason to trust me, a little boy, to properly use and return his tools. But my dad had that level of righteousness—he would use the tools correctly—and I was there in his name, so old Mr. Hanlan honored my requests.

David understood this. When he called

out, "O God of my righteousness," David was appropriating God's righteousness and applying it to himself by faith. It is not absolutely necessary to end each prayer by saying, "In the name of Jesus." But a confident supplicant has the understanding and faith that God has made Christ to be our righteousness (1 Corinthians 1:30). Anyone who often prays rejoices that "[God] hath made [Christ] to be sin for us, who knew no sin; that we might be made the righteousness of God in him" (2 Corinthians 5:21).

GIVE

ear to my words, O LORD,
consider my meditation.
Hearken unto the voice of my cry,
my King, and my God:
for unto thee will I pray.
My voice shalt thou hear
in the morning, O LORD;
in the morning will I direct
my prayer unto thee, and will look up.

PSALM 5:1–3

I USED
TO THINK
THAT PRAYER SHOULD

be spontaneous, spoken aloud directly from
my heart to God's. But not everyone can do
this. Not all people are verbal or eloquent, and
many feel prayer should be private, even
silent. Now I know that there are many ways
to pray. Psalm 5 shows three of these ways.

- *Give ear to my words.* What kind of
  words are these? Simple words spoken
  plainly are a familiar way of prayer.
  But words written down are prayer
  too. You might try this way when you
  are in a crowded place and desire fellowship with God. With paper and
  pen write your prayer to God.

  Words written well by others are
  also effective prayers. Here is one of
  my favorites adapted from the *Book of
  Common Prayer:*

  *"Most merciful God, I confess that I have
  sinned against you in thought, word,
  and deed, by what I have done, and by*

what I have left undone. I have not loved you with my whole heart; I have not loved my neighbor as myself. I am truly sorry and I humbly repent. For the sake of your Son Jesus Christ, have mercy on me and forgive me; that I may delight in your will, and walk in your ways, to the glory of your name. Amen."

- *Consider my meditation.* Prayer can be offered silently by way of thoughts. The way to do this is to invite God to consider your meditation just as the psalmist did. I sometimes turn thoughts of my children into such silent prayer.

- *Hearken unto the voice of my cry.* Is this a weeping cry? Is it crying out in anguish—or crying for joy? All of these can be given up to God as prayer. It does not matter how your prayers sound to the human ear. Only direct your prayer to God and look up with faith in divine love.

BUT

as for me, I will come into thy house
in the multitude of thy mercy:
and in thy fear will I worship
toward thy holy temple.
Lead me, O LORD, in thy righteousness
because of mine enemies;
make thy way straight before my face.

PSALM 5:7–8

WHAT GAVE DAVID THE ABILITY TO

pray? Was he a so-called prayer warrior? Not in his own eyes. David called his prayers sighing and crying (see Psalm 5:1–2 NRSV). He understood that boastful people have no place with God and knew the fate of evildoers, liars, the bloodthirsty, and deceivers (vv. 5–6). Surely David was better than such people. This must have given him the confidence to pray as he did.

But David didn't see it this way. How did he come to God's house, the house of prayer? What was his attitude? Did he come in the robes of the anointed king of Israel? In the armor of the leader of the armies of God? In other words, did he come in himself? No. He came in the multitude of God's mercy (v. 7). In one translation of this verse David says, "But I, through the abundance of your steadfast love, will enter your house" (NRSV).

In God's merciful love we are enabled to pray. Such love is entirely different than human love. It is much more substantial. God showed how much he loved us by sending his

Son, Jesus Christ, into the world. We have eternal life through Christ (see 1 John 4:9), and that life is a praying life.

David knew he was no better than the evildoers, liars, the bloodthirsty, and deceivers of his day. Likewise, a thousand years later, Paul wrote, ". . .nor thieves, nor covetous, nor drunkards, nor revilers, nor extortioners, shall inherit the kingdom of God. And such were some of you: but ye are washed, but ye are sanctified, but ye are justified in the name of the Lord Jesus, and by the Spirit of our God" (1 Corinthians 6:11). But since God loved us and sent his Son as a sacrifice to take away our sins (1 John 4:10), we now can pray our sighs and cries to God because we do not pray in ourselves, but in God's beloved Son.

WHEN

I consider thy heavens,
the work of thy fingers,
the moon and the stars,
which thou hast ordained;
what is man,
that thou art mindful of him?
and the son of man,
that thou visitest him?

PSALM 8:3–4

THERE WAS ONCE A ROMAN

philosopher and statesman by the name of Seneca (4 B.C.–A.D. 65). He was a contemporary of Jesus Christ and Rome's leading intellectual figure in the mid-first century. Seneca and his friends were the practical rulers of the Roman world between the years 54 and 62, during the first phase of the emperor Nero's reign. Seneca said,

> *"Is it to this little spot* [Rome] *that the great designs and vast desires of men are confined? Is it for this there is so much disturbance of nations, so much carnage, and so many ruinous wars? Oh, the folly of deceived men, to imagine great kingdoms in the compass of an atom, to raise armies to decide a point of earth with the sword!"*

The pride of man is the chief cause of war, devastation, slavery, desolation, and demoralization in this world. Yet, as the psalmist expresses, we are nearly nothing in proportion to the known universe. Earthly things like earthquakes, volcanoes, wind, and water, have their way with us while war, famine, and disease easily send us to the grave.

But for the labors of astronomers, we might never glimpse our insignificance amid the immensity of creation. Yes, we are the objects of God's loving care and mercy, yet each of us is physically little more than a grain of sand in the scheme of earth's history. Ours is such a small planet in its enormous solar system; what is it in the midst of the billions of galaxies teeming with blazing suns that fill the universe?

Yet God is mindful of us and even visited us as Jesus Christ. So every living woman and man should humbly join the centurion of Capernaum and say to him, "Lord, I am not worthy to have you come under my roof" (Matthew 8:8 NRSV). Yet when Jesus heard this, he was amazed at the man's humility, and said, "Truly I tell you, in no one in Israel have I found such faith" (v. 10 NRSV).

ARISE,

O LORD;
O God, lift up thine hand:
forget not the humble.
Wherefore doth the wicked contemn God?
he hath said in his heart,
Thou wilt not require it.
Thou hast seen it;
for thou beholdest mischief and spite,
to requite it with thy hand:
the poor committeth himself unto thee;
thou art the helper of the fatherless.

PSALM 10:12–14

THIS PSALM IS A PRAYER FOR

the poor, the helpless, and the oppressed. As it says in verse 2, "The wicked in his pride doth persecute the poor: let them be taken in the devices that they have imagined."

A person's attitude toward the needy is the litmus test of the Christian heart. In fact, amidst all the action and flashing light of truth in the Acts and Epistles, there is woven a continuous thread of charity for the poor. Even when Paul told about his important meeting with the leaders of the church in Jerusalem, he noted: "James, Peter and John. . .agreed that we should go to the Gentiles, and they to the Jews. All they asked was that we should continue to remember the poor, the very thing I was eager to do" (Galatians 2:9–10 NIV). The apostles did not only decide how to spread the gospel all over the earth; they were also eager to care for the needy.

In Antioch, the believers responded to a warning of famine by determining to send a contribution for the relief of the brothers and sisters living in Judea, and sent it in the care of

Barnabas and Paul (Acts 11:28–30). Later, Paul again delivered relief to Jerusalem, "For Macedonia and Achaia have been pleased to make a contribution for the poor among the saints in Jerusalem," he wrote. "Yes, they were pleased to do so" (Romans 15:26–27 NASB).

The apostle gave specific instructions about how to collect money for the poor: "As I directed the churches of Galatia, so do you also. On the first day of every week each one of you is to put aside and save, as he may prosper, so that no collections be made when I come" (1 Corinthians 16:1–2 NASB). And he boasted about the collection of money in the churches in Macedonia, calling this "the grace of God," and explaining, "in a great ordeal of affliction their abundance of joy and their deep poverty overflowed in the wealth of their liberality," Paul declared. "According to their ability, and beyond their ability they gave of their own accord, begging us with much entreaty for the favor of participation in the support of the saints" (2 Corinthians 8:1–4 NASB).

LORD,

thou hast heard the desire of the humble:
thou wilt prepare their heart,
thou wilt cause thine ear to hear:
to judge the fatherless and the oppressed,
that the man of the earth may no more oppress.

PSALM 10:17–18

Not
only is
Psalm 10

a prayer for the poor, it is a prayer against those who abuse and take advantage of them. If you carefully read the New Testament, you'll see the effect that Christ has on human charity, in contrast to what is seen in this psalm.

You'll see how the apostles were eager to care for the poor (Galatians 2:10). Moreover, the believers willingly determined to send aid to the poor in Jerusalem and were pleased to do so (Acts 11:29; Romans 15:26). Whole churches urgently gave beyond their ability (2 Corinthians 8:3–4). And when the apostle Paul told other churches about the generosity of the churches in Macedonia, he called it the grace of God.

God's grace is much more than a theological concept of unmerited favor to poor sinners. In the case of the generosity of the Macedonian churches, Paul uses the term to describe the expression of Christ in the believers. Likewise, he said that his apostolic work was not his own but the work of the grace of God that was with him (1 Corinthians 15:10). He didn't do it out of his human strength and ingenuity. In the same way, caring for the needy is not the natural inclination of the human life. Such charity expresses Christ.

The Gospels show that Jesus' disciples saw him express himself again and again. They were with him day and night; they'd seen him perform miracles and heard all of his marvelous teachings. They must have known him well and understood his expectations. Yet one day, encountering ten thousand hungry people, they found no charity in their own hearts. They said to Jesus, "Send the multitudes away, that they may go into the villages and buy themselves food" (Matthew 14:15 NKJV).

This is the natural rejoinder to the needs of the poor: "Let them take care of themselves; they are not my responsibility." But the response of Christ is, "You give them something to eat" (v. 16 NJKV). And the miracle that results is not just the feeding of the multitudes. Even more, it is the expression of the grace of God in charity through the human heart.

HELP,

LORD; for the godly man ceaseth;
for the faithful fail from
among the children of men.
They speak vanity every one with
his neighbour:
with flattering lips and
with a double heart do they speak.
The LORD shall cut off all flattering lips,
and the tongue that speaketh proud things. . . .

Thou shalt keep them, O LORD,
thou shalt preserve them
from this generation for ever.
The wicked walk on every side,
when the vilest men are exalted.

PSALM 12:1–3, 7–8

THIS PRAYER WAS PROBABLY COMPOSED

about three thousand years ago, and neighbors are lying to each other to this day, speaking with flattering lips out of insincere hearts. But notice how the prayer begins: *Help, Lord.*

"Help, Lord." How else can you pray when the world gives license for anyone to say, "I will lie to my hearts' content. My lips are my own—who can stop me?" (see Psalm 12:4 NLT). Certainly, the day will come when the Lord will bring flattery to an end and silence proud tongues (v. 3 NLT). In the meantime, what should we do? Psalm 12 speaks in the voice of God to give an answer: "I have seen violence done to the helpless, and I have heard the groans of the poor. Now I will rise up to rescue them, as they have longed for me to do" (v. 5 NLT).

You may have fallen prey to a liar. Insincerity may turn your stomach. Yet it is the helpless who are the victims of the world's duplicity. Children, the sick, the elderly, the uneducated all suffer most from such deceit. Righteousness responds to wickedness by showing charity to its victims. So if you have heard the groans of the poor, rise up to rescue them.

I HAVE

set the LORD always before me:
because he is at my right hand,
I shall not be moved.
Therefore my heart is glad,
and my glory rejoiceth:
my flesh also shall rest in hope. . . .

Thou wilt shew me the path of life:
in thy presence is fulness of joy;
at thy right hand there are
pleasures for evermore.

PSALM 16:8–9, 11

Hebrews 11
lists all kinds
of people who

were faithful to God. Early in this roster the author interjects, "For he that cometh to God must believe that he is, and that he is a rewarder of them that diligently seek him" (v. 6).

Surely the believers of Hebrews 11 were people who prayed in all kinds of ways. They made requests, applied for mercy, and gave thanks. They confessed and repented. They praised God. Yet there is another way of prayer that is not exercised as often as these. It is implied in Hebrews 11:6 that this way is practiced by those who diligently seek God— they believe that God is. The above verses from Psalm 16 mention this way of prayer: "I have set the LORD always before me. . . . Therefore my heart is glad."

Try this way of prayer. In your morning or evening prayer, instead of making requests or giving thanks or using other types of prayer, set the Lord before yourself like a table laden with food. In other words, repeat and proclaim all that the Lord is.

To do this, you may want to enlist the aid

of Scripture. There are many portions you can use. I like the section that begins with Colossians 1:15. Let's set the Lord before us with a few of these verses:

> *O Christ! You are the visible image of the invisible God. You existed before God made anything at all and you are supreme over all creation. I exult that you are the one through whom God created every-thing in heaven and earth—the things I can see and the things I can't see. Kings, kingdoms, rulers, and authorities— everything has been created through you and for you. I love you, Lord. You existed before everything else began, and you hold all creation together.*
> COLOSSIANS 1:15–17 (PARAPHASE)

This prayer sets the Lord before you. There can be thousands more like it. Each such prayer will make your heart glad and make you rejoice in God's glory. Moreover, such prayer causes the flesh to rest in hope and shows the way to the path of life.

I WILL
love thee,
O LORD,
my strength.

PSALM 18:1

"I LOVE YOU, LORD."

I believe this is the most profound prayer that can ever be spoken. It exposes other prayer as childish: "I want this or that"; and, "Do this or that."

Surely there is nothing wrong with being a child. As the apostle said, "When I was a child, I spoke like a child, I thought like a child, I reasoned like a child" (1 Corinthians 13:11 NRSV). After all, what else can a youngster do except be a child? All believers begin by speaking, thinking, and reasoning like the children in the faith that they are. But we each must eventually grow up to be mature in the faith. Then things change. Then, Paul says, we must put an end to childish ways.

Maturity is seen not in what one does; it is not in what one possesses. Maturity is seen in how one loves.

When my children were young, I was pleased to give them what they needed and, when possible, what they wanted as well. I liked to do as much for them as I could. But as they have grown into adulthood, all that has changed. I do little for them and give much less to them. They can take care of themselves. Yet I find I long for them to give me something. I want them to love me. That is all.

I am not saying that God and I share the same emotions. My example simply shows how I first loved my children and now I hope they will love me. Similarly, God's love was first revealed to us in this way: "God sent his only Son into the world so that we might live through him" (1 John 4:9 NRSV). By growing in the faith, we come to understand this love. And now, "We love because he first loved us" (v. 19 NRSV).

11

WITH

the merciful thou wilt shew thyself merciful;
with an upright man
thou wilt shew thyself upright;
with the pure thou wilt shew thyself pure;
and with the froward
thou wilt shew thyself froward.
For thou wilt save the afflicted people;
but wilt bring down high looks.
For thou wilt light my candle:
the LORD my God will enlighten my darkness.
For by thee I have run through a troop;
and by my God have I leaped over a wall.

PSALM 18:25–29

THIS
IS A PRAYER
OF REALIZATION.

Instead of asking God for something, sometimes you may tell in prayer what you love and
understand about God.

Remember the woman whom the scribes
and Pharisees caught in the act of adultery?
The story is found in John 8:1–11. After her
experience with Jesus, that woman could have
used this psalm for her prayer.

Those Pharisees were not really concerned
about the woman's sin. They were trying to
trap Jesus. They thought he would either con-
tradict the Law of Moses or participate in the
execution of the adulterer. Either way, they
hoped to cause his downfall. Instead, here is
what Jesus did: To the crooked he showed
himself to be shrewd (see Psalm 18:26 NIV).

"If any one of you is without sin, let him
be the first to throw a stone at her," he said
(John 8:7 NIV). This caused the Pharisees to
see that they too were sinners. As they slunk
away, Jesus saved the humble woman and
brought low those who had arrogant eyes. He
said to the woman, " 'Where are your accusers?

Didn't even one of them condemn you?'

" 'No, Lord,' she said. And Jesus said, 'Neither do I. Go and sin no more' " (John 8:10–11 NLT).

Now, how was it possible for this woman to do as the Lord said and "go and sin no more"? The answer is found in verse 12. Jesus said, "I am the light of the world. Whoever follows me will never walk in darkness but will have the light of life" (John 8:12 NRSV). When the adulterous woman encountered Christ, he lit her candle (Psalm 18:28); he enlightened her darkness with the light of life, and she realized who he was. This changed her life and enabled her to give up sin, run through a troop, and leap over a wall (v. 29). In other words, she was enabled to go and sin no more.

12

Who

can understand his errors?
cleanse thou me from secret faults.
Keep back thy servant also
from presumptuous sins;
let them not have dominion over me:
then shall I be upright,
and I shall be innocent from
the great transgression.
Let the words of my mouth,
and the meditation of my heart,
be acceptable in thy sight,
O Lord, my strength,
and my redeemer.

PSALM 19:12–14

THIS PRAYER IS AN HONEST RESPONSE

to the hymn that precedes it in verses 7–11—
a paean to the law of God. "The law of the
LORD is perfect, reviving the soul," sings the
poet. "The decrees of the LORD are trust-
worthy, making wise the simple" (v. 7 NLT).
And on he goes, telling all he can of the glo-
ries of God's commandments and ordinances.
"More to be desired are they than gold, yea,
than much fine gold: sweeter also than honey
and the honeycomb" (v. 10).

And he continues, "Moreover by them is
thy servant warned: and in keeping of them
there is great reward" (v. 11). Then the psalmist pauses and ponders the fact that, although
the law of God is perfect, he himself is not. So
naturally, he asks, "How can I know all the
sins lurking in my heart?" The answer is that
he cannot know this, nor can anyone else. So
he throws himself upon God's grace and mercy,
praying, "Cleanse me from these hidden
faults" (v. 12 NLT).

The prayer of Psalm 19:12–14 teaches
that the keeping of any law, no matter how

glorious, cannot save us. Why? Because our sinful nature is too weak to come up to the law's requirements. However, the sinful nature still thinks it is good enough to match the righteousness expressed in God's law. But God knows better than this and so sent his Son in a human body like ours, except without sin. Then God destroyed sin's control over us by giving the Son as a sacrifice for sin. This fulfilled the requirement of the law for us (Romans 8:3–4).

So, what do we do now? First, don't follow the sinful nature and attempt to keep the law on your own. Second, follow the Spirit by faith, because it is in the Spirit that the words of your mouth and the meditation of your heart are acceptable in the sight of God, your strength and your redeemer (Psalm 19:14).

13

MY

God, my God, why hast thou forsaken me?
why art thou so far from helping me,
and from the words of my roaring?
O my God, I cry in the daytime,
but thou hearest not;
and in the night season, and am not silent.
But thou art holy,
O thou that inhabitest the praises of Israel.
Our fathers trusted in thee:
they trusted, and thou didst deliver them.
They cried unto thee, and were delivered:
they trusted in thee, and were not confounded.

PSALM 22:1–5

HERE
IS THE
PSALM OF

the Cross. Psalm 22 in its entirety is a photograph of Christ's saddest hours and the record of his dying words. You can hear the New Testament echo of this ancient cry to God in Matthew 27:46. Jesus was hanging on the cross when "at about three o'clock, [he] called out with a loud voice, 'Eli, Eli, lema sabachthani?' which means, 'My God, my God, why have you forsaken me?' " (NLT). Jesus was forsaken by God because he bore our sin, the very sin that had separated us from God.

The remainder of the psalm is a poetic description of the dark suffering and the glory of the cross. There the man of sorrows prays until his speech fails him and he can only moan and groan like the helpless roaring of a wounded animal. "Why art thou so far from helping me, and from the words of my roaring?" he asks (v. 1). Is it possible to imagine Christ's anguish in seeing his own Father standing far off, neither helping nor apparently hearing? No, this is not possible. Yet those people who rest in Jesus Christ, the one who died as their substitute, know the reason this had to happen.

Remember how Jesus taught that "men ought always to pray, and not to faint" (Luke 18:1)? Here he practices what he preached. "O my God, I cry in the daytime, but thou hearest not" (v. 2). The day of his death was hurried and horrible, yet beginning from Gethsemane, he continued to pray even though no comfortable answer ever came.

So Jesus turned to praise: "But thou art holy, O thou that inhabitest the praises of Israel" (v. 3), and he used God's own holiness as the basis for his petition. Then, as if reminding both himself and God of the divine faithfulness, Christ remembered his faithful ancestors, who "trusted in thee: they trusted, and thou didst deliver them. They cried unto thee, and were delivered: they trusted in thee, and were not confounded" (vv. 4–5). And in three days Jesus Christ arose from the dead.

14

THOU

preparest a table before me
in the presence of mine enemies:
thou anointest my head with oil;
my cup runneth over.
Surely goodness and mercy shall follow me
all the days of my life:
and I will dwell in the house
of the LORD for ever.

PSALM 23:5–6

WHILE WALKING ON A WINTER'S STREET,

have you ever happened to see a door opened for someone to enter a warm house? For a moment the light streams out while genial music and welcoming voices are heard. Then the door quickly shuts; yet all that the eye, the ear, the heart, and the imagination have seen remain in you. Likewise, the Twenty-third Psalm is a moment's opening of David's soul, which radiates truths of peace and consolation that will never be absent from the world. This is how the American clergyman Henry Ward Beecher (1813–1887) described the Twenty-third Psalm.

Psalm 23 follows Psalm 22, which is sometimes called the Psalm of the Cross. There are no green pastures and no still waters there. Yet it is only after you read, "My God, my God, why hast thou forsaken me?" that you are blessed with the knowledge that "The LORD is my shepherd; I shall not want." This means that one must, through experience, know the value of Christ's blood spilled for redemption—one must, by revelation, see the spear pierce the man of sorrows. Out of this death comes the resurrection seen in Psalm 23, where we are served a peaceful feast at the shepherd's table.

And this is not a hasty bite of food. Instead the shepherd *prepares* a table for you. Nothing is hurried. The enemy is at your door, yet the table is neatly set and you are free to sit there and eat in peace. As you eat, Christ anoints your head with fragrant oil, just as he himself was once lovingly anointed—an act of great respect and love for a distinguished guest (Matthew 26:6–7).

All this, with the overflowing cup and the journey through life accompanied by goodness and mercy, are the believer's inheritance, bequeathed by the crucified and resurrected Christ.

15

Unto

thee, O Lord, do I lift up my soul.
O my God, I trust in thee:
let me not be ashamed,
let not mine enemies triumph over me.
Yea, let none that wait on thee be ashamed.

Psalm 25:1–3

THERE IS A HYMN I LOVE,

written by the British missionary M. E. Barber. It is about the church's longing for Christ's return. Ms. Barber penned the second verse of her hymn in a way that seems to echo the plea of Psalm 25:3: "Let none that wait on thee be ashamed."

> *Saint after saint on earth*
> *has lived and loved and died;*
> *And as they left us one by one,*
> *we laid them side by side;*
> *We laid them down to sleep,*
> *but not in hope forlorn;*
> *We laid them but to ripen there,*
> *till the last glorious morn.*

Believers have been looking forward to Christ's return ever since the disciples sat with Jesus on the Mount of Olives: "Tell us," they said, ". . .what will be the sign of your coming and of the end of the age?" (Matthew 24:3 NIV). How many generations have passed away from then to now? Each has been laid in graves in hope of Christ's return.

And those in this generation who await his appearing can pray with the psalmist, "Unto thee, O LORD, do I lift up my soul. O my God, I trust in thee: let me not be ashamed, let not mine enemies triumph over me" (vv. 1–2). We pray with Ms. Barber:

> *Come, Lord, and wipe away*
> *the curse, the sin, the stain,*
> *And make this blighted world of ours*
> *Thine own fair world again.*

And we can proclaim with the apostle Paul, "There is reserved for me the crown of righteousness, which the Lord, the righteous judge, will give me on that day, and not only to me but also to all who have longed for his appearing" (2 Timothy 4:8 NRSV).

16
SHEW

me thy ways, O LORD; teach me thy paths.
Lead me in thy truth, and teach me:
for thou art the God of my salvation;
on thee do I wait all the day.

PSALM 25:4–5

THE
PROMISE
OF THE NEW

covenant is that "they shall not teach every man his neighbour, and every man his brother, saying, Know the Lord: for all shall know me, from the least to the greatest" (Hebrews 8:11). In this spirit, the prayer of Psalm 25 is very personal—"Shew *me* thy ways, O LORD; teach *me* thy paths. Lead *me* in thy truth, and teach *me*"(italics added). Each Christian must personally learn the Lord's way. No one can teach it to you except God.

Notice that the prayer is not, "Shew me *my* ways, O LORD; teach me *my* paths." The way of a Christian is God's way, and that way is the same for all, yet each must learn the way personally.

Here is how to find the way: "Stand at the crossroads and look; ask for the ancient paths, ask where the good way is, and walk in it, and you will find rest for your souls" (Jeremiah 6:16 NIV). First, stand still, then look. Finally, ask for the ancient paths, the good way. Remember, you are not looking for a new or unique way. Then, as you walk in that way, you'll find rest for your soul (Matthew 11:28). This peaceful rest tells you you're walking on the godly pathway.

When people seek another way, they are burning "incense to worthless idols, which made them stumble in their ways and in the ancient paths" (Jeremiah 18:15 NIV). So Jeremiah advises, "Set up road signs; put up guideposts. Take note of the highway, the road that you take" (31:21 NIV).

Each Christian must personally learn the Lord's way, and the way to find that way is simply to ask; just as the disciple Thomas once asked, "Lord, . . .how can we know the way?" Jesus' answer is very simple, "I am the way" (John 14:5–6 NRSV).

17

I WILL

wash mine hands in innocency:
so will I compass thine altar, O LORD:
That I may publish with
the voice of thanksgiving,
and tell of all thy wondrous works.
LORD, I have loved the habitation of thy house,
and the place where thine honour dwelleth.

PSALM 26:6–8

IN THE ANCIENT DAYS, WHEN

a priest entered the tabernacle of God, his first act was to wash at the laver—a large basin of water. Then he was sanctified and could go to the altar and offer sacrifices to God. A believer today does the same while serving God in prayer because Christ, in his love for the church, has provided a way for this cleansing: He gave himself up for the church in order to make her holy with the washing of the water in the Word (Ephesians 5:25–27).

The Bible is the church's laver where she is washed with a kind of water that sanctifies her thoughts. Then in prayer she easily finds a voice of thanksgiving for all of Christ's wonderful works.

The Chinese-born evangelist Watchman Nee (1903–1972) once told about a woman who came to him complaining that she could not remember what she read in the Bible. He asked if she had ever washed rice in a colander or sieve. Of course she had.

"Do you try to keep the water in the sieve?" Nee asked.

"No," the woman replied, "that's impossible. Only the clean rice remains after the water washes through it."

"So it is as you read the Bible; your mind is made holy by the washing of the water in the Word."

There are two ways a Christian is made holy for service in prayer. First, once and for all by the blood of Christ who gave himself up for the church. Second, daily by the washing of the water in the Word. Continuing in these ways, our lives become the psalmist's prayer—"I have loved the habitation of thy house, and the place where thine honour dwelleth" (Psalm 26:8). And so Christ will present the church to himself as a glorious church holy and without fault, with no spot or wrinkle or any other blemish (Ephesians 5:27).

18

HEAR,

O LORD, when I cry with my voice:
have mercy also upon me, and answer me.
When thou saidst, Seek ye my face;
my heart said unto thee,
Thy face, LORD, will I seek.

PSALM 27:7–8

How
Does A
Person Seek

the face of Jesus Christ? Our example of this, as usual, is the apostle Paul, who said that he once forgave someone "in the presence of Christ" (2 Corinthians 2:10 NRSV). When you are in someone's presence, you can see that person's face and eyes. This is what Paul experienced.

Scholars know this by studying Greek, the language in which the New Testament was originally written. Simply put, they found that the word translated as *presence* in 2 Corinthians 2:10 is a form of the Greek word from which the English word *optical* originates; optical indicates *eyes*. This means that Paul sought the Lord's face, Christ's eyes, when forgiving others and no doubt at other times as well.

You may say, "This is too far out." It is in fact mystical. But the psalmist heard the words, "Seek the LORD and his strength, seek his face continually" (1 Chronicles 16:11), and responded saying, "Thy face, LORD, will I seek." Paul simply followed along this way and appealed to us to imitate him (1 Corinthians 4:16; 11:1). So, the experience of the face of

Christ is not beyond any of us—it is a part of the Christian life.

It is the experience that begins a person's Christian life. Here's how: One believes because that person has seen "the light of the gospel of the glory of Christ, who is the image of God" (2 Corinthians 4:4 NRSV). People who do not believe are much like believers except for one thing: The god of this world has blinded their minds to keep them from seeing the light of the gospel—the face of Jesus Christ (v. 4). So if you want to help people believe in Christ, ardently pray that God will remove the blinding veil from their minds.

As the apostle says, "It is the [same] God who said, 'Let light shine out of darkness' [Genesis 1:3], who has shone in our hearts to give the. . .knowledge of the glory of God in the face of Jesus Christ" (v. 6 NRSV).

19

THOU

hast turned for me
my mourning into dancing:
thou hast put off my sackcloth,
and girded me with gladness;
to the end that my glory
may sing praise to thee,
and not be silent.
O LORD my God,
I will give thanks unto thee for ever.

PSALM 30:11–12

Psalm 30 is a Wonderful Praise to God for

answered prayer. It is said to have been sung at the dedication of David's house in Jerusalem. In the midst of its exultation, the psalm reveals the prayer that was offered and answered: "I cried to thee, O LORD; and unto the LORD I made supplication. What profit is there in my blood, when I go down to the pit? Shall the dust praise thee? shall it declare thy truth? Hear, O LORD, and have mercy upon me: LORD, be thou my helper" (vv. 8–10).

David, called "a man after God's own heart" (see 1 Samuel 13:14), was the one who prayed this prayer. Can you see how it would be hard for God not to answer it? David's prayer teaches us how to pray prayers that will be answered. David prayed not with self-interest but according to God's heart. He prayed for what God wanted. Of course, the dust could not praise God or declare the truth. But David certainly could.

Moses prayed in the same way. When the people of Israel refused to go into the Promised Land as the Lord wished, they wept and cried and said, "Let us choose a captain, and go back to Egypt" (Numbers 14:4 NRSV). So God told Moses, "I will strike them with pestilence and disinherit them" (v. 12 NRSV).

But Moses reasoned with God. He told him that the nations who heard of him would say, " 'It is because the LORD was not able to bring this people into the land he swore to give them that he has slaughtered them in the wilderness' " (v. 15–16 NRSV).

" 'Forgive the iniquity of this people,' " Moses prayed, " 'according to the greatness of your steadfast love.'. . . Then the LORD said, 'I do forgive, just as you have asked' " (vv. 19–20 NRSV).

We also can pray such effective prayers. There is no reason not to model our modern prayers after those of the ancients and pray according to God's heart; God's greatness, righteousness, and love; God's own vital needs. Such prayers will be answered.

20

HAVE

mercy upon me, O LORD, for I am in trouble:
mine eye is consumed with grief,
yea, my soul and my belly.
For my life is spent with grief,
and my years with sighing:
my strength faileth because of mine iniquity,
and my bones are consumed. . . .

But I trusted in thee, O LORD:
I said, Thou art my God.
My times are in thy hand:
deliver me from the hand of mine enemies,
and from them that persecute me.
Make thy face to shine upon thy servant:
save me for thy mercies' sake.

PSALM 31:9–10, 14–16

SOME CHRISTIANS HAVE ENEMIES

like the enemies of King David—people who would kill them if they could. But usually we are our own worst enemy. So if you pray, "Deliver me from the hand of mine enemies, and from them that persecute me," you are likely praying for deliverance from your own thoughts and deeds.

The goal of the gospel is the transformation of the believer. According to Romans 12:2, this transformation is accomplished by the renewing of the mind. And this renewing comes through the Word, the Bible, the written gospel message. In other words, when you understand the gospel, your thinking changes.

The most thorough and seamless presentation of the gospel is found in the book of Romans. It begins with the creation of the world (1:20) and ends with the glorious freedom of the children of God (8:21) and the salvation of Israel (11:26). It reveals the full spectrum of salvation, including God's righteousness (chapters 1–2), the righteousness that is ours through faith (chapters 3–4), the results of righteousness (chapters 5–7), and life in the Spirit (chapter 8). To be sure, Romans is more than this. It probes the depth of the riches and wisdom and knowledge of God. "How unsearchable are his judgments and how inscrutable his ways!" (11:33 NRSV).

The author of Romans, the apostle Paul, ends his gospel message with this plea: "I appeal to you therefore, brothers and sisters, by the mercies of God, to present your bodies as a living sacrifice, holy and acceptable to God, which is your spiritual worship. Do not be conformed to this world, but be transformed by the renewing of your minds, so that you may discern what is the will of God—what is good and acceptable and perfect" (Romans 12:1–2 NRSV).

This renewing of the mind by the truth of the gospel is the way God delivers you from your worst enemy, yourself.

21

FOR

day and night thy hand was heavy upon me:
my moisture is turned into
the drought of summer.
I acknowledged my sin unto thee,
and mine iniquity have I not hid.
I said, I will confess
my transgressions unto the LORD;
and thou forgavest the iniquity of my sin.

PSALM 32:4–5

PEOPLE DON'T LIKE TO TALK ABOUT

sin. It is not a subject that is raised often, even among Christians. True, sin is negative. Yet the confession of sin is a wondrous thing; it is the beginning of prayer.

Remember the words of John: "If we say that we have no sin, we deceive ourselves, and the truth is not in us. If we confess our sins, he who is faithful and just will forgive us our sins and cleanse us from all unrighteousness" (1 John 1:8–9 NRSV).

David didn't need John to tell him this. "I confess my iniquity," he wrote. "I am sorry for my sin" (Psalm 38:18 NRSV). It seems to me that this was automatic for David. Confession was his habit. So he said in Psalm 32, "I will confess my transgressions unto the Lord; and thou for-gavest the iniquity of my sin" (v. 5). Then he continued, telling us all to do the same: "There-fore let all who are faithful offer prayer to you; at a time of distress, the rush of mighty waters shall not reach them" (v. 6 NRSV).

This habit of David's, his acknowledgment of sin and his telling of it to God, led him into a place we all must hope to know. "You are a hiding place for me," said Israel's king (v. 7 NRSV). It is as if David entered God's person through his confession and prayer. God was a place where he could hide and be preserved from trouble and be surrounded with glad cries of deliverance.

So too our confession makes us justified by faith. "We have peace with God through our Lord Jesus Christ: by whom also we have access by faith into this grace wherein we stand, and rejoice in hope of the glory of God" (Romans 5:1–2).

22

LOOK

to him, and be radiant;
so your faces shall never be ashamed.

PSALM 34:5 NRSV

THIS
SINGLE
VERSE IS AN

astounding encouragement to pray. It says that if you look to God you will be radiant. The New Testament strongly supports this claim.

During the times of the exodus of Israel, Moses was the only person who could meet with God, who could look to the Lord. This exposure to God's glory caused Moses' skin to shine, so he covered his face with a veil (Exodus 34:29–35). Second Corinthians 3 tells of this veil. It also says that if Moses' ministry of the law had glory, the New Testament ministry of the Spirit is much more glorious (vv. 7–11).

The ministry of Moses brought condemnation, but "now the Lord is the Spirit, and where the Spirit of the Lord is, there is freedom" (2 Corinthians 3:17 NRSV). Freedom to do what? Freedom to look to the Lord. "And all of us," says the Scripture, "with unveiled faces, seeing the glory of the Lord as though reflected in a mirror, are being transformed into the same image from one degree of glory to another; for this comes from the Lord, the Spirit" (v. 18 NRSV).

It is important to note these three words—"all of us." Before, it was only Moses who could go to the Lord. Later, this privilege belonged only to Israel's priestly class. But now the good news is that all of us can see the glory of the Lord. No one is more or less qualified to look to God. The question is, will you partake of this privilege?

If so, the promise of Psalm 34:5 will come to you. You will be "transformed into the same image from one degree of glory to another." No matter what your age or the color or condition of your complexion, you will be radiant.

23

THY

mercy, O LORD, is in the heavens;
and thy faithfulness reacheth unto the clouds.
Thy righteousness is like the great mountains;
thy judgments are a great deep: O LORD,
thou preservest man and beast.
How excellent is thy lovingkindness, O God!
therefore the children of men put their trust
under the shadow of thy wings.
They shall be abundantly satisfied
with the fatness of thy house;
and thou shalt make them drink
of the river of thy pleasures.
For with thee is the fountain of life:
in thy light shall we see light.

PSALM 36:5–9

You
MAY NOTICE
WHEN READING THE

prayers of the book of Psalms that when the psalmist is focused on himself he is miserable. But, without fail, when he looks at God all is well. This is the secret to laying aside the weight of this life and the sin that clings so close: Look away to Jesus, "the pioneer and perfecter of [your] faith" (Hebrews 12:2 NRSV).

Try this as you pray at the end of your day: Instead of asking for things, give thanks to the Father for sending the Son. List all you can remember of who Christ is and what he has done. Instead of pleading, speak praises to God. The effect of such prayer on your soul will astonish you.

This portion of Psalm 36 is such a prayer. Read it; even pray it. Its lyric comes directly from the Garden of Eden, where the food is the tree of life, and the refreshing river of God's pleasure is the fountain of life and the light of life. These thoughts and prayers of the psalmist are entirely outside this sad world.

Prayers like this project you forward into the city of hope—the New Jerusalem (Revelation

21:1–2). There you drink of a pure river of water of life, clear as crystal, which issues out of the throne of God and of the Lamb. In the middle of the city's single street and growing on either side of the river is the tree of life, which bears twelve different kinds of fruit. Its yield is ripe every month and its leaves heal all the nations of the earth. There is no night there, so you don't need a lamp or even the light of the sun. The Lord God gives you light. And there you reign forever and ever (Revelation 22:1–2, 5).

24

WITHHOLD

not thou thy tender mercies from me, O LORD:
let thy lovingkindness and
thy truth continually preserve me.
For innumerable evils have
compassed me about:
mine iniquities have taken hold upon me,
so that I am not able to look up;
they are more than the hairs of mine head:
therefore my heart faileth me.
Be pleased, O LORD, to deliver me:
O LORD, make haste to help me.

PSALM 40:11–13

DAVID IS IN BIG TROUBLE.

His crimes have taken hold on him and are more numerous than the hairs on his head, and he has no more heart to live. In reality, this should be everyone's prayer. The truth is, everyone on earth is under the power of sin (Romans 3:9). This is frightening.

What is sin? It is anything that divides you from God and from your fellowman. The Scriptures say, "No one is good—not even one. No one has real understanding; no one is seeking God. All have turned away from God; all have gone wrong. No one does good, not even one. Their talk is foul, like the stench from an open grave. Their speech is filled with lies. The poison of a deadly snake drips from their lips. Their mouths are full of cursing and bitterness. They are quick to commit murder. Wherever they go, destruction and misery follow them. They do not know what true peace is. They have no fear of God to restrain them" (Romans 3:10–18 NLT).

The psalmist understood these things and was fearful. This is why he said, "My heart faileth me." But the psalmist also knew there was one, and only one, with power over this sinful mess. And so he asked, "Be pleased, O LORD, to deliver me: O LORD, make haste to help me." This is the one way to overcome sin.

This is why when a troubled man asked long ago, "What must I do to be saved?" he was directed to the only one who would make haste to help him. "Believe on the Lord Jesus Christ," he was told, "and you will be saved, you and your household" (Acts 16:30–31 NKJV).

25

As

the hart panteth after the water brooks,
so panteth my soul after thee, O God.
My soul thirsteth for God, for the living God:
when shall I come and appear before God?

PSALM 42:1–2

THE SIMPLE WORDS OF

Psalm 42 tell of a simple pleasure—the thirst-quenching delight of fresh, cool water—but with a difference: Here, that water symbolizes the living God. Have you discovered the enjoyment of God in prayer? Yes, God can be enjoyed.

Charles Wesley knew this. He was an eighteenth-century British Methodist who wrote some 8,000 hymns, including "Hark the Herald Angels Sing," "Christ the Lord Is Risen Today," and "O for a Thousand Tongues to Sing." One of the less well-known of Wesley's hymns is "Our Hearts Are Full of Christ"—two verses set to an old English melody. Here is the second verse of this hymn:

> *Fairer than all the earthborn race,*
> *perfect in comeliness thou are;*
> *Replenished are thy lips with grace,*
> *and full of love thy tender heart.*
> *God ever-blest! We bow the knee,*
> *and own all fullness dwells in thee.*

Very few things are timeless, but this beautiful word sketch stirs the ancient impulse to enjoy the Lord. Unlike Wesley, not many people speak of such enjoyment today.

However, over 350 years ago the newly written Shorter Westminster Catechism mentioned this enjoyment of God. The catechism was written to instruct children in the Christian faith. Composed of 107 questions and answers, it is a brief introduction to the rule and essence of religion. It is still used today by English-speaking Presbyterians and by some Congregationalists and Baptists.

The first question asked in the catechism teaches the enjoyment of God. Discover this joy and find pleasure.

Question 1: What is the chief end of man?
Answer: Man's chief end is to glorify God, and to enjoy him forever.

26

WHY

art thou cast down, O my soul?
and why art thou disquieted in me?
hope thou in God:
for I shall yet praise him
for the help of his countenance.
O my God, my soul is cast down within me:
therefore will I remember thee
from the land of Jordan,
and of the Hermonites, from the hill Mizar.
Deep calleth unto deep
at the noise of thy waterspouts:
all thy waves and thy billows are gone over me.
Yet the LORD will command his
lovingkindness in the daytime,
and in the night his song shall be with me,
and my prayer unto the God of my life.

PSALM 42:5–8

THIS
IS THE LAMENT
OF A MAN WHO

is cut off from the worship of God, which to him is a refreshing, flowing stream for his soul (Psalm 42:1); it is as vital to him as water is to the body. But something prevents him from going to Jerusalem for the festivals (v. 4), so his tears flow instead of the cool stream (v. 3).

Whatever is keeping the psalmist from God, he sees it as a conspiracy of deep calling to deep like a violent waterspout that connects dark storm clouds above with raging sea below (v. 7). To his ears this call sounds like the thundering cataracts of a falling river. What's more, "All thy waves and thy billows are gone over me"—one after another, troubles overwhelm him. Despite all this, there exists the buoyancy of God's loving-kindness, and out of nowhere a song comes up in this believer's heart (v. 8).

When this psalm was written, there was only one place to worship God: Jerusalem. The psalmist's life was nearly ruined because he was prevented from worshipping there. But those days are past. The time has come when true worshippers worship the Father in spirit and in truth. Nothing prevents this. The Father is looking for anyone who will worship him this way (John 4:23). There is no correct physical location to love and worship and enjoy the Lord because God is Spirit, and those who worship him "worship him in spirit and in truth" (v. 24).

27

O SEND

out thy light and thy truth:
let them lead me;
let them bring me unto thy holy hill,
and to thy tabernacles.

PSALM 43:3

THIS
VERSE
COMMUNICATES

a tremendous request to God. "O send out thy light and thy truth: let them lead me." Is it possible that God would not answer this prayer? I don't think so.

I have often prayed a prayer that lends utterance to these few words of Psalm 43. It is the prayer of Ephesians 1:17–21. And I think that God may be answering. When I pray this prayer I personalize the words of Scripture, making the request for myself. Below is a version that you may wish to use for yourself. Please, be my guest.

O God of my Lord Jesus Christ, Father of glory, give me a spirit of wisdom and revelation as I come to know you more and more. Enlighten the eyes of my heart so that I can know the hope to which you have called me; and so that I can know the great riches of your glorious inheritance among the saints.

Do this, O God, according to the working of your great power. Answer

*my prayer with the power that you put
to work in Christ when you raised him
from the dead and seated him at your
side in the heavenly places far above all
rule and authority and power and
dominion, and above every name that is
named. Thank you, Lord. Amen.*

I have confidence to pray like this because
these are not my words. They do not contain
my ideas. These are words derived directly from
Scripture. Surely God desires that you and I
would have a spirit of wisdom and revelation;
that we would have enlightened hearts and live
in the hope of our calling. Not only so, in the
midst of the seeming endless prayers for blessings, what greater riches are there than that of
God's inheritance among the saints?

28

GOD

is our refuge and strength,
a very present help in trouble.
Therefore will not we fear,
though the earth be removed,
and though the mountains be carried
into the midst of the sea;
though the waters thereof roar and be troubled,
though the mountains shake
with the swelling thereof.

PSALM 46:1–3

New York's World Trade Center towers have

been attacked. They've collapsed into the streets. America is reeling and the death toll is rising. The community of lower Manhattan has been visited by an event that some say is of biblical proportions. It was as if the earth was removed in a moment. We wince and reel at the sight of it. Mountains tremble in the midst of the sea—the waters roar and are troubled.

I am mourning—mourning for the people who have suddenly, simultaneously lost their lives. I weep for the bereaved and the children who are all at once motherless or fatherless.

America—the greatest empire the world has yet seen—is rallying in righteous anger, invoking God's blessing. Our country is organizing the world to war against those who have done this hideous thing and others who may wish to commit similar unspeakable acts of mass murder. As we do this, I imagine history's kingdoms and empires looking on in mute witness.

There are the shadows of Persia and Babylon. Nearby stand the sun kings of Egypt.

Alexander the Great and the emperor-gods of Rome have gathered. The British Union Jack, the flag upon which the sun never set, snaps somewhere in the breeze, and the Soviet Union shivers, rising a bit from frozen ground to see what can be seen.

There is David, king of Israel, resting on the hillside. He holds a harp and softly sings songs that few can hear. Their lyrics tell of an eternal kingdom with a ruler named the Prince of Peace.

Harp strings ring while David chants:

God is our refuge and strength
a very present help in trouble.
Therefore will we not fear
though the waters roar and foam.

There is a river, the streams thereof
shall make glad the city of God,
the holy place of the tabernacles
of the Most High.

29

GREAT

is the LORD,
and greatly to be praised in the city of our God,
in the mountain of his holiness.
Beautiful for situation,
the joy of the whole earth, is mount Zion,
on the sides of the north,
the city of the great King. . . .

We have thought of thy lovingkindness,
O God, in the midst of thy temple.
According to thy name, O God,
so is thy praise unto the ends of the earth:
thy right hand is full of righteousness.

PSALM 48:1–2, 9–10

GREAT IS THE LORD IN THE CITY OF OUR GOD!

God's greatness is beyond comprehension. God is greater than man (Job 33:12), the greatest of all (Psalm 95:3), and greatness itself (145:3). This psalm of praise locates the great and infinite God in an actual, physical location. The English poet John Milton (1608–1674) called this place

> *Fair Jerusalem*
> *The Holy City, lifted high her towers,*
> *And higher yet the glorious temple reared*
> *Her pile, far off appearing like a mount*
> *Of alabaster, topt with golden spires.*
> From *Paradise Regained*

Ancient Jerusalem rose above deep valleys on its west, south, and east. It could only be militarily attacked from the northwest—the sides of the north—where it was magnificently fortified by walls, towers, and bulwarks. These were the wonder and dread of the nations. The psalmist reports that the kings of the earth joined forces and advanced against the city. But when they saw it, they were stunned and ran away gripped with terror, like a woman writhing in the pain of childbirth or like mighty ships being shattered by a powerful wind (Psalm 48:4–7).

The Old Testament saints loved Jerusalem and thought about it always. They would never forget this wonder of God. But what did they actually meditate upon? "We have thought of thy lovingkindness, O God" (v. 9).

What does one think of when considering God's loving-kindness? Simply this: The infinite God was willingly limited to something finite. For the ancient Jews this was Jerusalem. It was the unique place where they could find God and offer their gifts of praise and thanksgiving. But in the modern day God is found in Jesus Christ, "who, being in the form of God, thought it not robbery to be equal with God: but made himself of no reputation, and took upon him the form of a servant, and was made in the likeness of men" (Philippians 2:6–7).

This man embodies God's loving-kindness to all the world (see John 3:16).

30

I WILL

not reprove thee for thy sacrifices
or thy burnt offerings,
[which are] continually before me.
I will take no bullock out of thy house,
nor he goats out of thy folds.
For every beast of the forest is mine,
and the cattle upon a thousand hills.

PSALM 50:8–10

IN THE OLD DAYS OF ISRAEL, THERE WERE

many ways of offering animals as sacrifices to God. These sacrifices were presented year after year in the same ways. Why? Because "under the law almost everything is purified with blood, and without the shedding of blood there is no forgiveness of sins" (Hebrews 9:22 NRSV).

Psalm 50 shows that despite all these sacrifices, something was wrong in Israel. The offerings were continually before God—plenty of blood was shed. This met the people's need for forgiveness of sins (v. 8), but it did not meet God's need. After all, every animal on earth already belongs to God (vv. 9–11).

But the psalmist told Israel to "offer to God a sacrifice of thanksgiving" (v. 14 NRSV). God did not only want their basic animal sacrifices. God wanted their hearts—their love.

Just like Israel, we have forgiveness of sins. In fact, we have more than this. Our sin is taken away. This is why the Scripture says that when Christ appeared, he *removed* sin by offering himself as the sacrifice, once for all (Hebrews 9:28). But this is just the beginning.

It sets the stage for us to move forward and meet God's need. So the book of Hebrews says, "Therefore let us go on toward maturity, leaving behind the basic teaching about Christ" (6:1 NRSV, see translation footnote).

The Gospel of Mark illustrates how to do this: A scribe wanted to know what the most important commandment might be (12:28). Today we would ask, "What is the most important thing I can do for God? Go to church? Give to the poor? Pray? Be a good citizen?"

The ancient scribe in Mark's Gospel gives us the right answer, "There is one God; . . .and to love him with all the heart, and with all the understanding, and with all the soul, and with all the strength, and to love [your] neighbour as [yourself], is more than all whole burnt offerings and sacrifices."

Jesus told the man, "Thou art not far off from the kingdom of God" (vv. 32–34).

31

HAVE

mercy upon me, O God,
according to thy lovingkindness:
according unto the multitude
of thy tender mercies
blot out my transgressions.
Wash me thoroughly from mine iniquity,
and cleanse me from my sin.
For I acknowledge my transgressions:
and my sin is ever before me.
Against thee, thee only, have I sinned,
and done this evil in thy sight:
that thou mightest be justified
when thou speakest,
and be clear when thou judgest.

PSALM 51:1–4

DAVID, THE KING OF ISRAEL, ONCE

committed a horrid series of sins, including adultery, murder, and deceit. You must read the story of his sin in 2 Samuel 11:1–12:25 to better appreciate why Psalm 51 has been called the "sinner's guide." Its prayer of repentance gives great help to people seeking to restore their fellowship with God.

Athanasius (A.D. 293–373), the hero of the Council of Nicea, recommended that Christians repeat Psalm 51 when they awake at night. And Martin Luther (A.D. 1483–1546) reported, "There is no other psalm which is more often sung or prayed in the church." Any amount of time spent pondering and praying these words will return a profit.

Severe problems can come up when your thoughts dwell on the multitude of your sins. Problems like self-condemnation, depression, defeat. So follow the guide of Psalm 51. It gives this comfort: Our God has a multitude of tender mercies. If we have as many sins as the hairs of our head, God's mercies number as the stars of the universe.

God is infinite. So God's mercies are infinite. And divine mercy is as far above human sin as God is above the sinner.

What then can you do? The sacrifice God wants from you is a broken spirit. God will not reject your repentant heart (Psalm 51:17). After all, "If we say that we have no sin, we deceive ourselves, and the truth is not in us. If we confess our sins, he is faithful and just to forgive us our sins, and to cleanse us from all unrighteousness" (1 John 1:8–9).

32

BUT

I am like a green olive tree
in the house of God.
I trust in the steadfast love
of God forever and ever.
I will thank you forever,
because of what you have done.
In the presence of the faithful
I will proclaim your name,
for it is good.

PSALM 52:8–9 NRSV

SEVEN
OUT OF THE
NINE VERSES IN

Psalm 52 compose a diatribe against someone who has done mischief against the godly—someone who plots destruction and works treachery (vv. 1–2). This person loves evil more than good, and lying more than speaking the truth (v. 3).

To such a person this severe warning is issued: "God will break you down forever; he will snatch and tear you from your tent; he will uproot you from the land of the living. The righteous will see, and fear, and will laugh at the evildoer" (vv. 5–6 NRSV).

There are plenty of people like this in the world—destructive, treacherous, even evil—though I've rarely met them. But when the righteous laugh at this evildoer they say, "See the one who would not take refuge in God, but trusted in abundant riches, and sought refuge in wealth!" (v. 7 NRSV). This surprises me.

Through most of the 1990s, the U.S. economy was booming, and people all around were discussing and investing in the stock market. At the same time, the post-World War II generation began retiring. So advertising and the media focused on money for retirement. Even more than usual, people—good people who go to church and park their sports utility vehicles in the parking lot—seem to trust in abundant riches and seek refuge in wealth.

As I said, I'm surprised at Psalm 52. It exposes destructive, treacherous, evil people and issues to them the most serious of warnings—"He will uproot you from the land of the living" (NRSV). But then it describes such people in a way that I recognize. Suddenly these could be my neighbors. In fact, Psalm 52:7 nearly describes the American Dream—they trust in riches and seek refuge in wealth.

They could be me!

33

SAVE

me, O God, by thy name,
and judge me by thy strength.
Hear my prayer, O God;
give ear to the words of my mouth.
For strangers are risen up against me,
and oppressors seek after my soul:
they have not set God before them.
Behold, God is mine helper:
the LORD is with them
that uphold my soul.
He shall reward evil unto mine enemies:
cut them off in thy truth.

PSALM 54:1–5

IF YOU
READ ABOUT
THE BACKGROUND

of this prayer in 1 Samuel 22–23 you'll see how vigorously David was being hunted by his enemies.

David's prayer in Psalm 54 reveals that he did not rush into conflict with Doeg the Edomite or the people of Keilah or the Ziphites. Instead, he first contended with God for blessing and help (vv. 1–3). Despite his formidable political and military skills, David didn't dare lift his hand against the enemies of God until he had first lifted up his hands in supplication to the Lord who had taught those hands to war, those fingers to fight (Psalm 144:1).

"Hear my prayer, O God," begged the king, because he knew that if he had God's ear he could not be overcome by trouble. Other tactics may fail, but not prayer. It is always available and effective.

Please note: This is not a rote prayer. Nor is it perfunctory. David's situation had become so dangerous that he could not afford to pray out of mere custom. He had to succeed in prayer or fall victim to his foes.

So with the unique confidence of a praying person, David spoke prophetically, promising himself victory with God's help (Psalm 54: 4–5). He is our example of prayer and faith, just like many others: "Gideon, Barak, Samson, Jephthah, . . .Samuel, and all the prophets. By faith these people overthrew kingdoms, ruled with justice, and received what God had promised them" (Hebrews 11:32–33 NLT).

34

As
for me, I will call upon God;
and the LORD shall save me.
Evening, and morning, and at noon,
will I pray, and cry aloud:
and he shall hear my voice.
He hath delivered my soul in peace
from the battle that was against me:
for there were many with me.
God shall hear, and afflict them,
even he that abideth of old.

PSALM 55:16–19

CONSIDER
THE CONDITION
OF DAVID WHEN HE

prayed: "My heart is in anguish within me; the terrors of death assail me. Fear and trembling have beset me; horror has overwhelmed me" (Psalm 55:4–5 NIV). A modern mental health professional might say that he was severely depressed and suffering an anxiety attack.

Perhaps he was. Seeking relief, he resorts to fantasy: "I said, 'Oh, that I had the wings of a dove! I would fly away and be at rest—I would flee far away and stay in the desert; I would hurry to my place of shelter, far from the tempest and storm' " (vv. 6–8 NIV). Translating this fantasy into modern terms, it reads, "Oh, that I had the winning lottery ticket! I would drive away in my new car—I would hurry to my new house, far from the tempest and storm."

Happily, the psalmist eventually did find his "wings of a dove" when he called upon God. Thousands of years later this is still the way of salvation. As the old hymn says, "Take the name of Jesus with you, child of sorrow and of woe. It will joy and comfort give you;

take it then, where'er you go."

The woman who wrote these words was Lydia Baxter (1809–1874), who was an invalid for much of her life. Nevertheless she had a cheery, reassuring disposition. Here's why: "I have a very special armor," she said. "I have the name of Jesus. When the tempter tries to make me blue or despondent, I mention the name of Jesus, and he can't get through to me anymore." So Baxter's friends reported that they didn't visit her sickroom for the usual reasons. Instead of giving comfort and care, they themselves received encouragement at her bedside.

The name of Jesus is a believer's passage out of woe, "For whosoever shall call upon the name of the Lord shall be saved" (Romans 10:13).

35

You

have kept count of my tossings;
put my tears in your bottle.
Are they not in your record?
Then my enemies will retreat
in the day when I call.
This I know, that God is for me.

PSALM 56:8–9 NRSV

A FATHER CARES FOR HIS SON IN WAYS DEEPER

than simple provision. Sure, he gives his son food and clothing and a warm house. But he thinks about his son's health, and worries about his schoolwork too. A father likes to watch his son play, and watches over his safety. He has to discipline his boy sometimes. Occasionally, a father's caring can turn to frustration and even anger because he cares so much. Ideally, after years of caring, a son will say, "This I know, that my dad is for me."

David, the author of Psalm 56, knew that God paid close attention to his life—counting how many times he tossed and turned in the night; collecting his tears and keeping a record of them. So David said, "This I know, that God is for me." God was for David for a good reason: In the far future, Jesus Christ the Messiah would be born out of David's family (Matthew 1:1).

Like a father with his son, God cares for you and me; and eventually we say, "This I know, that God is for me." But, as in David's case, God is for us for a reason—God has a purpose. Christ's coming out of David's family was a step in the completion of this purpose, as were Christ's death, resurrection, and ascension (Ephesians 3:11).

The next step has to do with us. The book of Romans says that all things work together for good for those people who are called according to God's purpose (8:28). Next it tells what is good: "For those whom he foreknew he also predestined to be conformed to the image of his Son" (v. 29 NRSV). If all the things that happen to me conform me to the image of God's Son, that's really good. And that's God's purpose. Eventually, Jesus Christ will be the firstborn Son in a large family composed of people like you and me (v. 29).

So, "what then are we to say about these things? If God is for us, who is against us?" (v. 31 NRSV).

36

Be

merciful unto me, O God,
be merciful unto me:
for my soul trusteth in thee:
yea, in the shadow of thy wings
will I make my refuge,
until these calamities be overpast.

PSALM 57:1

THE PSALMS ARE UNLIKE ANY OTHER PORTION OF THE

Bible because they are so personal. In them human voices talk directly to God. Time and again, they speak of finding refuge. And they find it, not in ordinary shelters, but in God.

Here in Psalm 57, the poet sees himself as a helpless chick in a brood of birds hiding under their mother's wings. She holds them close, snuggled against her warm, feathered body while a calamity passes over. Maybe this calamity is some bird of prey flying high above on the hunt. Or it could be a violent storm, the winds of which would scatter the young birds far from safety. This image of chicks sheltered by the wings of a hen is notable because it occurs frequently in Scripture—six times in the Psalms, twice in the Gospels, and once in Ruth.

Can you see the picture? You are a baby chicken—a little yellow one like those we see at Easter—and God is like a mother hen. This is not my idea. Jesus said it before me (Matthew 23:37). I'm sorry that more people don't hold this image of themselves and God.

Needless to say, God is God and unlike anything else. But people sometimes use metaphors and analogies to describe the various aspects of God. Some of these are drawn from the Bible. One image that is not from the Bible, yet may be the most common, is that of an angry old man with a gray beard, sitting on a storm cloud, casting lightning to earth.

True, God is the judge, and there will be anger in the day of judgment. But we must remember, and tell others, that today God is not a judge. Rather, God is like a mother hen, and he desires to gather all people under his wings for warmth and safety (Matthew 23:37; see also 1 Timothy 2:4).

37

You
have set up a banner
for those who fear you,
to rally to it out of bowshot,
Give victory with your right hand,
and answer us,
so that those whom you love may be rescued.

PSALM 60:4–5 NRSV

DAVID WAS A WARRIOR,

and here he draws a picture taken from his experience in battle—the picture of a banner set up out of bow shot. If you rally around that banner, you are safe from the deadly arrows of your enemy. David also prays for victory and that those whom God loves would be rescued from danger.

Whom does God love? Everyone knows: "God so loved the world, that he gave his only begotten Son" (John 3:16). God loves everyone in the world. This love caused God to lift up Christ like a banner for people to rally to out of bow shot.

When did this happen? Jesus himself tells the story: "Just as Moses lifted up the serpent in the wilderness, so must the Son of Man be lifted up" (v. 14 NRSV).

When the people of Israel were traveling through the wilderness, they spoke against God. So poisonous snakes came and bit them. Many died. Then they repented and asked that the snakes would be taken away. God told Moses to make a serpent out of bronze and lift it up on a pole. "And whenever a serpent bit someone, that person would look at the serpent of bronze and live" (Numbers 21:4–9 NRSV).

The serpent that Moses lifted up foreshadowed Christ on the cross. It was made of bronze. It had the appearance of all the other serpents, except it had no poison. So it was with Jesus. He was just like all the rest of us except for one thing—he had no sin. So Scripture says that the Son was sent from God in the likeness of sinful flesh (Romans 8:3). Then he was lifted up on the cross where "for our sake [God] made him to be sin who knew no sin" (2 Corinthians 5:21 NRSV).

There he is, Christ crucified! Can you see him there? He is God's beautiful banner set up safely out of bow shot. When, on the battlefield of this world, people rally to him, they are healed of sin and become "the righteousness of God in him" (2 Corinthians 5:21).

38

Hear

my cry, O God; attend unto my prayer.
From the end of the earth will I cry unto thee,
when my heart is overwhelmed:
lead me to the rock that is higher than I.
For thou hast been a shelter for me,
and a strong tower from the enemy.
I will abide in thy tabernacle for ever:
I will trust in the covert of thy wings.

Psalm 61:1–4

I LOVE
THE PRAYER
"LEAD ME TO

the rock that is higher than I" (v. 2). It is poetic and helpless and childlike. Though this rock is the Lord Jesus Christ, people have difficulty finding and approaching him; sheltering and resting in him. We have doubts and fears. Pride and self obscure the way. Both religion and the world blind and distract us.

So be lenient if you overhear someone pray in a half-unbelieving, bewildered way; praying a prayer like the publican in Luke 18. "Standing afar off, [he] would not lift up so much as his eyes unto heaven, but smote upon his breast, saying, God be merciful to me a sinner" (v. 13). His heart may have been like the psalmist's, overwhelmed, bordering on despair.

God is truly formidable and seems to be a high, hard rock. The prodigal son probably felt this way about his father. So he prayed, "Father, I have sinned against heaven, and in thy sight, and am no more worthy to be called thy son" (Luke 15:21).

But here is why we can find sweet shelter

in the rock. The rock is a man: "And a man shall be as an hiding place from the wind, and a covert from the tempest; as rivers of water in a dry place, as the shadow of a great rock in a weary land" (Isaiah 32:2).

This is Christ in whom "all the fullness of God was pleased to dwell, and through him God was pleased to reconcile to himself all things, whether on earth or in heaven, by making peace through the blood of his cross" (Colossians 1:19–20 NRSV).

An old hymn tells of this man, this refuge, this rock that is higher than I am; the rock that is so high that it casts over all things the cool shade of God's pleasure in Christ Jesus:

> *O, safe to the rock*
>   *that is higher than I,*
> *My soul in its conflicts*
>   *and sorrows would fly,*
> *So sinful, so weary,*
>   *thine, thine would I be,*
> *Thou blest Rock of Ages,*
>   *I'm hiding in thee.*

WILLIAM O. CUSHING (1823–1902)

39

O GOD,

thou art my God;
early will I seek thee:
my soul thirsteth for thee,
my flesh longeth for thee
in a dry and thirsty land,
where no water is.

PSALM 63:1

"MY SOUL THIRSTETH FOR THEE."

The human soul is a thirsty thing, not unlike the human body. Both dry up and die without water. We recognize the signals that our bodies send when they are thirsty. Then, the thing to give them is pure water. This best slakes thirst.

The soul is thirsty too. But its water is not physical. "My soul thirsteth for God, for the living God," sang the psalmist (Psalm 42:2). God is water to the human soul. We must drink this water or our soul withers. So the Lord promised, "I will pour water on the thirsty land, and streams on the dry ground; I will pour my spirit upon your descendants, and my blessing on your offspring" (Isaiah 44:3 NRSV). The Spirit of God is the drink that satisfies the soul. In fact "we were all made to drink of one Spirit" (1 Corinthians 12:13 NRSV).

Somehow David knew that his soul would not be satisfied by drinking anything other than God's Spirit. As king, he could freely sample so many pleasures of this life.

Maybe this is how he found that this world is "a dry and thirsty land, where no water is" (Psalm 63:1).

What are the signals that say my soul is thirsty? Anger, frustration, sadness—these are some. What are some others? Each of us should make a list. Confusion, blame, deceit—these too are signs of thirst. A general sense of dissatisfaction is easy to recognize as thirst. Oh, that when these arise in our souls, we would recognize them as the call to drink the Spirit of God: "Ho, every one that thirsteth, come ye to the waters, and he that hath no money; come ye, buy, and eat; yea, come, buy wine and milk without money and without price" (Isaiah 55:1).

40

THOU

visitest the earth, and waterest it:
thou greatly enrichest it with the river of God,
which is full of water:
thou preparest them corn,
when thou hast so provided for it.
Thou waterest the ridges thereof abundantly:
thou settlest the furrows thereof:
thou makest it soft with showers:
thou blessest the springing thereof.
Thou crownest the year with thy goodness;
and thy paths drop fatness.
They drop upon the pastures of the wilderness:
and the little hills rejoice on every side.
The pastures are clothed with flocks;
the valleys also are covered over with corn;
they shout for joy, they also sing.

PSALM 65:9–13

PSALM 65
IS LIKE A DEWY, FRESH MORNING.

Its final five verses are a succession of pastoral images—a description in natural figures of "the tender mercy of our God; whereby the dayspring from on high hath visited us, to give light to them that sit in darkness and in the shadow of death, to guide our feet into the way of peace" (Luke 1:78–79).

Look at the scene sketched in the psalmist's verses: The earth is prepared and seed is provided to the sower. The seasonal rain waters the seed ridges, settles the furrows, and softens the seed. The seed swells, germinates, and springs from the soil. Then the year is crowned with a harvest that is so abundant that its fruit overflows the reapers' wagons and drops along the paths. The hillsides, covered with flocks, echo with joyous shouts and singing from the fruitful valley.

This is the image of answered prayer. After the anguished appeals of earlier psalms, all is well because God has answered. Such things do happen to people who pray.

Remember Jesus' story of a rich man who

had a fertile farm that produced so much that his barns were full to overflowing? That farmer was so self-satisfied that he sat back and said to himself, "I have enough stored away for years to come. Now take it easy! Eat, drink, and be merry!" (see Luke 12:15–20). What a contrast to this psalm. In it there is not one word of man, of man's skill, or man's labor. Not one thought of self. Instead the prayer is, "*Thou* visitest the earth. . . . *Thou* crownest the year with *thy* goodness."

Most Americans are far removed from the pleasant harvests of the agrarian past. Still, may God guide each of us on paths overflowing with the excess harvest of answered prayer.

41

I WILL

go into thy house with burnt offerings:
I will pay thee my vows,
which my lips have uttered,
and my mouth hath spoken,
when I was in trouble.
I will offer unto thee burnt sacrifices of fatlings,
with the incense of rams;
I will offer bullocks with goats.

PSALM 66:13–15

THIS PSALM FLOODS US WITH A REPORT

of God's great works and gracious benefits. It is too much to deal with at once. The psalmist responds with promises of ample sacrifices— all kinds of big burnt offerings like rams and bullocks. Goats are the smallest thing he intends to give. Indeed, the doings of God that are recorded in the Old Testament are so amazing that they are almost beyond words. The psalmist probably thought all the bulls and rams in the world were not enough to adequately give thanks.

But we must take note of one event that goes beyond all this: God was born as a man (John 1:14). There is a poem that tells of this, Christina Rossetti's "In the Bleak Midwinter":

Our God, heaven cannot hold him,
nor earth sustain;
Heaven and earth shall flee away
when he comes to reign;
In the bleak midwinter a stable
place sufficed
The Lord God Almighty, Jesus Christ.

Nothing so important had been done since the completion of creation. Is there an offering that is adequate in response to this act of God? Rossetti says,

What can I give him, poor as I am?
If I were a shepherd, I would bring a lamb;
If I were a wise man, I would do my part;
Yet what I can give him: give my heart.

There is nothing more to do but give ourselves to God. All the rest has been done in Christ. Let's all now pay our vows to the Lord in the presence of his people, asking, "What shall I render unto the LORD for all his benefits toward me? I will take the cup of salvation, and call upon the name of the LORD" (Psalm 116:12–13).

42

BUT

as for me, my prayer is unto thee, O LORD,
in an acceptable time: O God,
in the multitude of thy mercy hear me,
in the truth of thy salvation.
Deliver me out of the mire,
and let me not sink:
let me be delivered from them that hate me,
and out of the deep waters.
Let not the waterflood overflow me,
neither let the deep swallow me up,
and let not the pit shut her mouth upon me.

PSALM 69:13–15

A WELL
IS A WONDERFUL
PLACE WHERE WATER IS

brought forth. But what is a well that goes dry? It is nothing more than a pit. In the ancient Middle East, when wells no longer yielded water they were sometimes used as pit prisons, with no care taken to clean out the miry mud remaining at the bottom.

For example, when Jerusalem was besieged by the armies of Babylon, Jeremiah predicted that those who stayed in Jerusalem would die, while those who surrendered to the Babylonians would live (Jeremiah 38:2). City officials told the king, "Sir, this man must die! That kind of talk will undermine the morale of the few fighting men we have left" (v. 4 NLT). So they "took Jeremiah from his cell and lowered him by ropes into an empty cistern in the prison yard. . . . There was no water in the cistern, but there was a thick layer of mud at the bottom, and Jeremiah sank down into it" (v. 6 NLT).

Scholars say that such wells were capped by masonry, and often a large stone was available to close the aperture. To shut the mouth of a well was to move this stone over its opening. So when the poor prisoner prayed, "Let not the pit shut her mouth upon me" (Psalm 69:15), he was begging that he would not be buried alive in a dry well.

This desperate man's prayer is a pattern for anyone stuck in the mire of life. "But as for me, my prayer is unto thee, O LORD, in an acceptable time: O God, in the multitude of thy mercy hear me, in the truth of thy salvation. Deliver me out of the mire" (vv. 13–14).

43

HEAR

me, O LORD;
for thy lovingkindness is good:
turn unto me according to
the multitude of thy tender mercies.
And hide not thy face from thy servant;
for I am in trouble: hear me speedily.
Draw nigh unto my soul, and redeem it:
deliver me because of mine enemies.

PSALM 69:16–18

ONE DAY, GOD TOLD ABRAHAM,

"I have heard that the people of Sodom and Gomorrah are extremely evil. . . . I am going down to see whether or not these reports are true." (Genesis 18:20–21 NLT). Abraham knew this meant those cities were going to be destroyed. The problem was that Abraham had relatives in Sodom—his nephew Lot and his family. So Abraham prayed.

In his prayer, Abraham did a remarkable job of bargaining with God. He convinced the Lord to not destroy Sodom and Gomorrah if there were even ten righteous people living there (Genesis 18:23–33). How did he do this? He prayed according to God's own righteousness. Abraham knew that because God is righteous, it is impossible for righteous people to be destroyed in divine judgment.

David, praying in Psalm 69, does the same. He is in big trouble, imprisoned in either an actual or figurative pit. He is afraid that someone is going to seal the mouth of that pit and bury him alive (v. 15). So he prays, "O God, in the multitude of thy mercy hear me, in the truth of thy salvation. Deliver me out of the mire" (vv. 13–14). He doesn't make a list of reasons why he should be saved. Rather he appeals to God's multitudinous mercy and invokes the truth of God's salvation. Then he commands, "Hear me, O Lord" (v. 16).

Who could be so brash with God? Anyone who knows God's love can be so confident. The psalmist issues God a second reminder about the abundance of divine mercy, and continues with his prayer (v. 16).

Today, we also can pray with great, even brash, confidence because "we have peace with God through our Lord Jesus Christ" (Romans 5:1). All the appeals of the Old Testament saints are wrapped up in Christ—righteousness, love, mercy, and the truth of salvation. In your prayer, invoke the one name, Jesus, and you'll have "access by faith into this grace wherein we stand, and rejoice in hope of the glory of God" (v. 2).

44

IN

thee, O LORD, do I put my trust:
let me never be put to confusion.
Deliver me in thy righteousness,
and cause me to escape:
incline thine ear unto me,
and save me.
Be thou my strong habitation,
whereunto I may continually resort.

PSALM 71:1–3

THIS SUMMER I VISITED THE GRAVES OF

my grandfather and grandmother. I had often stayed in their house when I was a boy. But now that house is gone, and so are my grandparents. Their house was temporal and the bodies in which they lived were temporary.

Here the psalmist prays for a permanent home. "Be thou my strong habitation." Have you ever heard anyone pray words like these? *O God, be my house, be my home, be my dwelling place.* I know that Christ wants to make my heart into his home. I've even prayed for this according to Ephesians 3:17: "That Christ may dwell in your hearts through faith." But to have my home in God? This is beyond anything I imagined when I first believed. *O Lord, be thou my strong habitation, whereunto I may continually resort.*

When Sarah died, Abraham confessed that he was a stranger and a sojourner among the people in the land (Genesis 23:4). And Moses said, "I have been a stranger in a strange land" (Exodus 2:22). God told the Hebrews that they were strangers and sojourners in the land

(Leviticus 25:23). And David himself confessed this was true (Psalm 39:12). Our progenitors in the faith considered themselves homeless.

Early on, Moses stated the truth that they all must have known: "LORD, thou hast been our dwelling place in all generations" (Psalm 90:1). So when Abraham by faith "dwelt in the land of promise as in a foreign country, dwelling in tents" (Hebrews 11:9 NKJV), he actually had a home. He was dwelling in God.

And now I want to make David's prayer my own: *O Lord, be thou my strong habitation, whereunto I may continually resort.* And I want to become more like Abraham who "looked for a city which hath foundations, whose builder and maker is God" (v. 10)

45

THOU

shalt guide me with thy counsel,
and afterward receive me to glory.
Whom have I in heaven but thee?
and there is none upon earth
that I desire beside thee.

PSALM 73:24–25

JESUS CHRIST ONCE SAID, "YOUR EYE IS

the lamp of your body. If your eye is healthy, your whole body is full of light" (Luke 11:34 NRSV). A person with a healthy eye can see where he is going and is not easily distracted from his goal.

Yet there are so many excellent distractions!

For example, blessings. There are spiritual blessings—gifts of healing, insight, self-expression; physical blessings—health, stature, appearance; and personal blessings—family, employment, housing. And how about feelings? Happiness, satisfaction, peace, joy, etc. Or activities—church service, prayer, Bible study, giving of time and money.

Every one of these things is good. Yet not one of them is Christ. True, these blessings can have their source in God, but if one seeks such blessings, he has been diverted from the goal of the faith. Christ is himself the blessing. The psalmist knew this. So he prayed, "Whom have I in heaven but thee? and there is none upon earth that I desire beside thee."

For example, when you journey home at

Thanksgiving, is your goal a turkey dinner? Not really. Home is the goal even if there is no Thanksgiving meal waiting there. As the poet Christina Rossetti once wrote,

> *Thou are thyself my goal, O LORD my King:*
> *Stretch forth thy hand to save my soul:*
> *What matters more or less of journeying?*
> *While I touch thee I touch my goal,*
> *O Sweet Jesu.*

Consider Paul—if anyone was blessed, it was he: "Circumcised on the eighth day, a member of the people of Israel, of the tribe of Benjamin, a Hebrew born of Hebrews; as to the law, a Pharisee; as to zeal, a persecutor of the church; as to righteousness under the law, blameless" (Philippians 3:5–6 NRSV). Paul let all this go for one reason: "Whatever gains I had, these I have come to regard as loss because of the surpassing value of knowing Christ Jesus my Lord. . . . This one thing I do: forgetting what lies behind and straining forward to what lies ahead, I press on toward the goal for the prize of the heavenly call of God in Christ Jesus" (vv. 7–8, 13–14 NRSV).

46

FOR

God is my King of old,
working salvation in the midst of the earth.
Thou didst divide the sea by thy strength:
thou brakest the heads of
the dragons in the waters.
Thou brakest the heads of leviathan in pieces,
and gavest him to be meat to
the people inhabiting the wilderness.
Thou didst cleave the fountain and the flood:
thou driedst up mighty rivers.
The day is thine, the night also is thine:
thou hast prepared the light and the sun.
Thou hast set all the borders of the earth:
thou hast made summer and winter.

PSALM 74:12–17

THIS PORTION OF THE BIBLE TELLS AN

old, old story. There's a song written by Katherine Hankey (1834–1911) and published in 1872 that also talks about that beloved story. Here's the first verse:

Tell me the old, old story
of unseen things above,
Of Jesus and his glory,
of Jesus and his love.
Tell me the story simply,
as to a little child;
For I am weak and weary,
and helpless and defiled.

Miss Hankey followed the lead of the poets who wrote the book of Psalms. They frequently told the story of Israel's deliverance from Egypt, the Exodus through Sinai, and the rest of the history of the chosen race (Psalm 78; 105; 106; 114:1–4; 135:8–12; 136; 137:1–6). In doing this, they attended to God's warning to "be very careful never to forget what you have seen the LORD do for you.

Do not let these things escape from your mind as long as you live! And be sure to pass them on to your children and grandchildren" (Deuteronomy 4:9 NLT).

"Tell me the story slowly, that I may take it in," sings Hankey. "That wonderful redemption, God's remedy for sin." But people have let the story of God's remedy for sin escape from their mind. Even Miss Hankey, in the last verse of her song, says she is afraid that "this world's glory is costing me too dear."

Here's the old story that must not "escape from your mind as long as you live! And be sure to pass [it] on to your children and grandchildren" (Deuteronomy 4:9 NLT). Sin—that ugly divide between God and the human race—is destroyed by Christ's death (Romans 8:3). So we Christians are dead to sin (6:11). But this does not make us that much better than our neighbors. We don't have a more pure form of politics. We are not in better health than others. Our struggles, successes, and failures are the same. Yet we tell an old story that is always new: We are dead to sin—the divide between us and God is bridged in Christ—and we are alive to God through Jesus Christ our Lord (6:11).

47

O DELIVER

*not the soul of thy turtledove
unto the multitude of the wicked:
forget not the congregation of
thy poor for ever.
Have respect unto the covenant:
for the dark places of the earth
are full of the habitations of cruelty.*

PSALM 74:19–20

THE SETTING OF PSALM 74 IS THE

destruction of the first temple in Jerusalem. "They set your sanctuary on fire," the poet cries. "They desecrated the dwelling place of your name, bringing it to the ground. . . . They burned all the meeting places of God in the land. We do not see our emblems; there is no longer any prophet" (vv. 7–9 NRSV). If you believed in God in those days, all was lost. God's habitation had been overrun by the hordes of the outside world.

But the poet is also a prophet. He reminds God of all that divine power had done: The light and the sun were prepared, all the bounds of the earth were decided, summer and winter were made (vv. 16–17). He then reminds God of the turtledove, God's beloved Israel. Today the turtledove is also God's believers in the church. It represents those who love the Lord (Song of Solomon 5:2).

All around us, people scoff at that love. The impious revile the name Jesus. Why? Because, as in the ancient time, the habitation of God's testimony is razed to the ground.

The prayer in days like this must be like the psalmist's, "Do not deliver the soul of your dove to the wild animals" (Psalm 74:19 NRSV). To me this means, "Don't let my soul become like theirs."

We must pray to the one who prepared the light and the sun, decided the bounds of the earth, and made summer and winter: *Have regard for your covenant, and be a God to us and to our offspring* (see v. 20; Genesis 17:7).

48

O REMEMBER

not against us former iniquities:
let thy tender mercies speedily prevent us:
for we are brought very low.
Help us, O God of our salvation,
for the glory of thy name:
and deliver us, and purge away our sins,
for thy name's sake.

PSALM 79:8–9

THIS PSALM READS LIKE ONE OF JEREMIAH'S

laments amid the ruins of Jerusalem. It is a time of invasion, oppression, and overthrow in Israel. The poet is weeping over the greatest calamity, "They have defiled your holy temple," he cries (Psalm 79:1 NRSV). This means that the true worship of God was extinguished—a cause of greatest grief. At the heart of this lament is the prayer of repentance in verses eight and nine.

Why do you say, "I'm sorry" to people you've hurt or offended? So you can be comfortable with them again, talk with them, and have the benefit of their companionship. Fellowship is broken by offenses and repaired by apology. This is the lesson to be learned by the destruction of the temple.

If someone avoids you because you did or said something careless, it is not, strictly speaking, a punishment. Rather, it is the natural result of your offense—a wall suddenly exists between the two of you. Israel, in various ways, had offended God. The entire nation had sinned. This created a barrier that eliminated all possibility of divine fellowship—that is to say, worship was no longer possible—the temple was gone.

When you feel cold toward God, indifferent; when you have no fellowship with the Lord, perhaps an offense has created a barrier between you and your God. The temple within you has been, if not destroyed, at least locked, shuttered, darkened. The thing to do is say you're sorry.

It is a deception to claim fellowship with God but tolerate such darkness. But through repentance like the psalmist's, the light that is Christ returns. The temple reopens. Fellowship with God and with others is restored because the blood of Jesus cleanses us from every sin.

"If we say we have no sin, we are only fooling ourselves and refusing to accept the truth. But if we confess our sins to him, he is faithful and just to forgive us and to cleanse us from every wrong" (1 John 1:8–9 NLT).

49

GIVE

ear, O Shepherd of Israel,
thou that leadest Joseph like a flock;
thou that dwellest between
the cherubims, shine forth.
Before Ephraim and Benjamin
and Manasseh stir up thy strength,
and come and save us.
Turn us again, O God,
and cause thy face to shine;
and we shall be saved.

PSALM 80:1–3

How
SHALL WE
PRAY FOR THOSE

who cannot pray for themselves? When the people of Israel were far from God, they had prophets to pray for them. Psalm 80 shows how one of these prophets prayed. The words of the first verse of this prayer show the way. That is, pray according to who God is.

The prophet of Psalm 80 first prays to God, who is a Shepherd leading a flock. Israel desperately needed their Shepherd-God. So three times the prayer asks the Shepherd, "Turn us again" (vv. 3, 7, 19). This is what a shepherd sometimes does—he turns the flock toward the pasture for food and to a stream for water. A shepherd will turn a flock away from danger and also turn it around to return to the fold. Scripture reveals God as a Shepherd (Psalm 23:1; Isaiah 40:11), so the psalmist prays to God the Shepherd, "Turn us again."

This prayer also addresses God who dwells between the cherubim (v. 1). In the ancient days, Israel worshipped God at the Tabernacle. There, above the lid of the ark of the covenant, were two gold cherubim. Between these cherubim, under the shadow of their wings, was where God's glory shone the brightest. This is where God was when meeting with Israel's high priest (Exodus 25:18–22).

Israel was in darkness at the time this psalm was composed. Its poet-prophet knew that Israel needed bright light to expose the people's sin and show them the way. So he prayed, not to God in general, but to God who dwelt between the cherubs. Four times his prayer asks God to shine on Israel (vv. 1, 3, 7, 19).

How should we pray? Seek to know the one to whom we pray (Philippians 3:10). Then we will pray as did the prophets before us.

50

How

amiable are thy tabernacles, O LORD of hosts!
My soul longeth, yea,
even fainteth for the courts of the LORD:
my heart and my flesh crieth out
for the living God.
Yea, the sparrow hath found an house,
and the swallow a nest for herself,
where she may lay her young,
even thine altars, O LORD of hosts,
my King, and my God.
Blessed are they that dwell in thy house:
they will be still praising thee.

PSALM 84:1–4

A
SPARROW'S NEST
IN THE ALTAR OF

the tabernacle is impossible except in the mind of a poet. That altar was a place for slaughter. A vulture would love to live there, not a sparrow. Yet here you have little sparrows and swallows flitting about the altar, laying eggs, and raising little birds. Remember, this is poetry, and poetry often deals with another reality, something unseen. By the same token, our faith also tells us of things we cannot see (Hebrews 11:1).

It tells us things about Christ: He is the visible image of the invisible God, who existed before God made anything at all; the one through whom God created everything in heaven and earth. Christ is the one who holds all creation together and is the head of the church, his body. He is the first of all those who will rise from the dead. In fact, he is first in everything.

The fullness of God was pleased to dwell in Christ. And by him everything in heaven and on earth is reconciled to God. And (here is where we get back to the sparrows and the altar) God made peace with everything by means of Christ's blood on the cross (Colossians 1:15–20).

That cross was a place of slaughter too. It was the most violent, degrading, and ugly way of punishment that Roman authorities could devise. It is where Jesus died and where God made peace with man. This is why the apostle Paul, speaking like a sparrow, said, "As for me, God forbid that I should boast about anything except the cross of our Lord Jesus Christ" (Galatians 6:14 NLT).

By appearances, that cross, that altar, was repulsive, something from which to flee. But faith sees it as does the Scotswoman Elizabeth Clephane (1830–1869)—a delightful place of peace, a place to rest:

Beneath the cross of Jesus
I fain would take my stand,
The shadow of a mighty rock
within a weary land;
A home within the wilderness,
a rest upon the way,
From the burning of the noonday heat,
and the burden of the day.

51

Bow

down thine ear, O Lord,
hear me: for I am poor and needy.
Preserve my soul; for I am holy:
O thou my God,
save thy servant that trusteth in thee.
Be merciful unto me, O Lord:
for I cry unto thee daily.
Rejoice the soul of thy servant:
for unto thee, O Lord, do I lift up my soul.
For thou, Lord, art good, and ready to forgive;
and plenteous in mercy unto
all them that call upon thee.
Give ear, O Lord, unto my prayer;
and attend to the voice of my supplications.

Psalm 86:1–6

JUST AS
PSALM 90
IS TITLED

"The Prayer of Moses," this psalm is known as David's prayer. As the celebrated English Baptist minister and preacher Charles Haddon Spurgeon (1834–1892) said, "David composed it, and no doubt often expressed himself in similar language; . . .the prayers of a good man have a family likeness, but they vary as much as they agree. We may learn from the present psalm that the great saints of old were accustomed to pray very much in the same fashion as we do; believers in all ages are of one genus [kind]."

This is why those who pray may often find themselves praying words much like these of David. And, if you are short of words for prayer, simply speak this prayer word for word—the Lord will bow down to hear you.

Are you like David—poor and needy? Then, Spurgeon says, you are "doubly a son of poverty, because, first, poor and without supply for [your] needs, and next needy, and so full of wants, though unable to supply them." Though David was the renowned king of

Israel, he knew his true condition—poor and needy—and was unashamed to admit it. He knew, as Spurgeon explains, "Our distress is a forcible reason for our being heard by the Lord God, merciful, and gracious, for misery is ever the master argument with mercy."

There is no need to be original when praying to God. "What has been will be again, what has been done will be done again; there is nothing new under the sun. Is there anything of which one can say, 'Look! This is something new'? It was here already, long ago; it was here before our time" (Ecclesiastes 1:9–10 NIV). So we are free to make David's prayer our own.

52

AMONG

the gods there is none like unto thee, O LORD;
neither are there any works like unto thy works.
All nations whom thou hast made shall come
and worship before thee, O LORD;
and shall glorify thy name.
For thou art great,
and doest wondrous things:
thou art God alone.

PSALM 86:8–10

HERE IS WHAT CHARLES HADDON SPURGEON

said about the prayer of Psalm 86: "This psalm consists of praise as well as prayer, but it is in all parts so directly addressed to God that it is most fitly called 'a prayer.' A prayer is none the less, but all the more, a prayer because veins of praise run through it."

These words are found in the *Treasury of David*, Charles Spurgeon's classic work on the book of Psalms. This monumental work was first published in weekly installments over a twenty-year period. Entire sections were released volume by volume until the seven-volume set was complete in 1885. More than 120,000 sets were sold before the turn of the twentieth century.

In the *Treasury of David*, Spurgeon addresses each psalm in three ways: *Exposition* gives his own verse-by-verse commentary. *Explanatory Notes and Quaint Sayings* calls on the published work of various other Bible teachers. And in the final section, *Hints to the Village Preacher*, Spurgeon briefly outlines topics and insights for each verse.

Charles Haddon Spurgeon was called "The Prince of Preachers." Thousands attended his early ministry in London at the New Park Street Chapel and then later in the new six thousand-seat Metropolitan Tabernacle. (Spurgeon selected the term *Tabernacle* because, as he said, "We believe this building to be temporary, meant for the time in the wilderness without the visible King.")

A genius of intellect, with natural gifts of oratory and biblical exposition, Spurgeon was greatly blessed by the Holy Spirit, so his many writings and sermons remain widely published. This includes his magnum opus, the *Treasury of David,* concerning which Spurgeon's wife remarked that if her husband had never written anything else, this would be his permanent literary memorial.

53

O LORD

God of my salvation,
I have cried day and night before thee:
let my prayer come before thee:
incline thine ear unto my cry;
for my soul is full of troubles:
and my life draweth nigh unto the grave.
I am counted with them that
go down into the pit:
I am as a man that hath no strength;
free among the dead,
like the slain that lie in the grave,
whom thou rememberest no more:
and they are cut off from thy hand.

PSALM 88:1–5

IF THERE EVER WAS A

song of sorrow, this is one. Psalm 88 is unique for the unrelieved gloom of its tone. This is not a hymn; it is a dirge from beginning to end.

Listen closely to this lament, and you will hear Christ's voice in his suffering. Jesus "emptied himself" of glory (Philippians 2:7 NRSV), and found his soul full of troubles (Psalm 88:3). He was the mighty God (Isaiah 9:6) who cried out, "I am as a man that hath no strength" (Psalm 88:4). He who is resurrection life (John 11:25) found himself among the dead (Psalm 88:5). Therefore, amazed, Jesus Christ agonized, "My God, my God, why have you forsaken me?" (Matthew 27:46 NIV; see also Psalm 88:5).

Sometimes you too may feel forsaken. At that time however, you are not like Christ; you are the prodigal son. He was cut off from his father and found himself feeding among the pigs (Luke 15:11–16). So too you may feel alienated from God.

The prodigal was not forsaken by his father. Rather, he purposely distanced himself from his father—his source of life and love. When one day he came to his senses and trudged along home, he rehearsed a prayer of despair: "Father, I have sinned against both heaven and you, and I am no longer worthy of being called your son. Please take me on as a hired man" (vv. 18–19 NLT). But this prayer would have no effect.

His father loved his son and had already forgiven him. He was looking for his son and saw him coming from far off. He ran and lovingly embraced the boy, who then began his prayer, "Father, I have sinned against both heaven and you." But the father wasn't listening. He interrupted his boy and gave instructions for a celebration to begin (15:22–24).

And when you remember the prodigal son, remember Jesus Christ as well. He was forsaken, cut off from God one time so the rest of us would not have to remain feeding with the pigs. God made Christ to be sin who knew no sin so that we could become the righteousness of God in him (2 Corinthians 5:21).

54

LORD,

thou hast been our dwelling place
in all generations.
Before the mountains were brought forth,
or ever thou hadst formed
the earth and the world,
even from everlasting to everlasting,
thou art God.
Thou turnest man to destruction; and sayest,
Return, ye children of men.
For a thousand years in thy sight are
but as yesterday when it is past,
and as a watch in the night.

PSALM 90:1–4

FROM THE REMOTE PAST, THE NAME

Moses has been attached to Psalm 90. Christian biblical scholars from Jerome (c. 347-420) forward have accepted this as a prayer of the "man of God." They cite its unique simplicity and grandeur and how it fits his era and situation. It resembles Moses' Law in connecting sin with death and is similar in expression to the poetic portions of the Pentateuch. Scholars point out that this psalm is unlike the psalms of David and those written later by others. In short, scholars find it difficult to consign Psalm 90 to any author other than Moses (c. 1400 B.C.).

If this is so, it is one of the oldest poems in the world. It makes Homer (c. 800–700 B.C.), the Greek epic poet and author of the *Odyssey*, relatively modern. And even King David's psalms, written around 1000 B.C., are recent in comparison—as modern as Robert Frost (1874–1963) is to Chaucer (1342–1400)—there are nearly five centuries between them.

In his prayer, Moses says that one thing remains changeless amid the perpetual change in the universe—the faithfulness of the everlasting to everlasting God. When Moses said this, was he thinking of the burning bush, the persecution in Egypt, the Red Sea, Pharaoh with his chariots of war, the weary march of Israel through the wilderness? Certainly, and in all of this he experienced that God "is the Rock, his work is perfect: for all his ways are judgment" (Deuteronomy 32:4).

Moses considered "the days of old, . . .the years of many generations" (v. 7) and saw that God has a dwelling place in all generations.

Let us do the same and look back to the days of Moses and Joshua and David, and the days of the human life of the Son of God; to Paul and Peter and all the saints of the church forward to the present. Moses could only call on a thousand years as testimony. We are more blessed than he because we have at least thirty-five hundred years that prove the Lord is the dwelling place of those that trust in him from generation to generation.

55

O SATISFY

us early with thy mercy;
that we may rejoice and be glad all our days.
Make us glad according to the days
wherein thou hast afflicted us,
and the years wherein we have seen evil.
Let thy work appear unto thy servants,
and thy glory unto their children.
And let the beauty of the LORD
our God be upon us:
and establish thou the work of
our hands upon us;
yea, the work of our hands establish thou it.

PSALM 90:14–17

THE
FINAL THOUGHT
OF THIS PRAYER—

perhaps an afterthought—is a request that God would bless the people's efforts: "Establish thou the work of our hands." Let's always ask for such blessing. But note that the psalmist first desired that "the beauty of the LORD our God be upon us" (v. 17).

The apostle Paul was a successful man in the religious world. It seems that, in the words of Psalm 90, the work of his hands had been established. He was born into a pure-blooded Jewish family that was a branch of the tribe of Benjamin—a real Jew if there ever was one. Plus he was a successful member of the Pharisees, the ancient sect that demanded the strictest obedience to the Jewish law. He was so zealous that he harshly persecuted the church—an aberrant sect of Judaism in Paul's day. He obeyed the Jewish law so carefully that he was never once accused of error. If he could succeed at this, he would prosper at whatever he tried (see Philippians 3:4–6).

Then one day Paul's measure of success changed. "I once thought all these things were so very important," he said. "But now I consider them worthless because of what Christ has done. Yes, everything else is worthless when compared with the priceless gain of knowing Christ Jesus my Lord" (vv. 7–8 NLT). The apostle discarded everything but the desire to know Christ. He considered everything else garbage. He only wanted to have Christ and become one with him (vv. 8–9). Then the beauty of the Lord would be upon him.

Paul then was no longer the successful man of his past. He had become more like the psalmist who sang, "One thing have I desired of the LORD, that will I seek after; that I may dwell in the house of the LORD all the days of my life, to behold the beauty of the LORD, and to inquire in his temple" (Psalm 27:4).

Forgetting the past, Paul was like a runner looking forward only to what lies ahead. He pressed toward what he considered to be success—the end of the race and the prize of the high calling of God in Christ Jesus (Philippians 3:13–14).

56

I͆t

is a good thing to give thanks unto the LORD,
and to sing praises unto thy name,
O most High:
to shew forth thy lovingkindness
in the morning,
and thy faithfulness every night,
upon an instrument of ten strings,
and upon the psaltery; upon the harp
with a solemn sound.
For thou, LORD, hast made me glad
through thy work:
I will triumph in the works of thy hands.

PSALM 92:1–4

I ONCE LIVED IN A PLACE IN

New England where the residual effects of so-called blue laws could still be seen. These laws mandated, among other things, that shops be closed on Sunday. They hearkened back to the days of the strict English Puritans who first settled the region. The Puritans were serious about keeping the Sabbath, which they observed on Sunday. So stores were closed on Sunday. Legislatures have repealed almost all the blue laws; but this has occurred only in the last thirty years.

Not that long ago, one didn't go shopping on Sunday because most stores weren't open. I'm no Puritan, but I liked this—it took some pressure off the day. I not only didn't have to go to work; I didn't have to go shopping either.

Psalm 92 is titled Song for the Sabbath Day. Read its first four verses. Aren't they relaxing, restful? They provide the mind with a brief sabbath. It is a good and healthy thing to stop thinking about your work from time to time. The psalmist knew this and so told the

Lord, "You, O LORD, have made me glad by *your* work" (v. 4 NRSV, italics added).

Allow yourself a moment's sabbath and forget your own work. Instead, think of God's work in creation. Think of the work of God's incarnation in Jesus Christ; the labor of redemption through Christ's death; the resurrection; the ascension of Jesus to the heavens; the work of the outpouring of the Holy Spirit. These are the ways God shows forth loving-kindness in the morning and faithfulness every night (v. 2).

Early in human history, God laid down this edict: "By the sweat of your face you shall eat bread until you return to the ground, for out of it you were taken" (Genesis 3:19 NRSV). Our rest is found in the work of God—"For thou, LORD, hast made me glad through thy work: I will triumph in the works of thy hands" (Psalm 92:4).

57

LET

the heavens rejoice, and let the earth be glad;
let the sea roar, and the fulness thereof.
Let the field be joyful, and all that is therein:
then shall all the trees of the wood
rejoice before the LORD:
for he cometh, for he cometh to judge the earth:
he shall judge the world with righteousness,
and the people with his truth.

PSALM 96:11–13; SEE ALSO 98:7–9

WHY
IS IT THAT
ONLY THE CREATION

celebrates the coming of Christ to the earth—at least in this account of it? These verses sketch quite a scene. Almost all things are mentioned —the heavens and earth, the sea and everything in it, the fields and the animals living in them, plus all the trees in the woods. These rejoice and are glad; they roar and are joyful.

Today the creation is in a different condition: "We know that the whole creation has been groaning in labor pains until now" (Romans 8:22 NRSV). Though it is in pain, it "waits with eager longing for the revealing of the children of God" (v. 19 NRSV).

When mankind fell away from God, the creation was unwillingly dragged along (v. 20). It was innocent of rebellion and did not sin against God. Still, our fall subjected it to futility and the bondage of decay (vv. 20–22).

Meanwhile, among the human race, children of God have been conceived through faith in Christ (John 1:12–13). Romans 8 shows that these people are growing to maturity, unseen, like a child in the womb. The whole creation is groaning like a woman in labor, longing and waiting for them to be revealed at the Lord's second coming. Then the creation will obtain the freedom of the glory of the children of God (v. 21).

Try to imagine the creation without death and decay. Now look at the creation that is with us today. It is but the ruin of the work of God's hands. The marvelous beauty seen in a sunset, a rainbow, a flower, a kitten is the residue of the creation's original glory.

Not only does the creation groan, but we also groan inwardly while we wait for adoption, the redemption of our bodies. What this will be has not been revealed. What we do know is this: When Christ is revealed, we will be like him (1 John 3:2). After all, "he who did not withhold his own Son, but gave him up for all of us, will he not with him also give us everything else?" (Romans 8:32 NRSV).

58

BLESS

the LORD, O my soul:
and all that is within me, bless his holy name.
Bless the LORD, O my soul,
and forget not all his benefits:
who forgiveth all thine iniquities;
who healeth all thy diseases;
who redeemeth thy life from destruction;
who crowneth thee with lovingkindness
and tender mercies;
who satisfieth thy mouth with good things;
so that thy youth is renewed like the eagle's.

PSALM 103:1–5

THE
FIRST SENTENCE
OF THIS PSALM SHOWS

the poet using his will to control his soul. I think that he had somehow learned the hard lesson that those who live according to the flesh think about the flesh, but those who live by the Spirit think about the things of the Spirit (see Romans 8:5).

This lesson teaches that our flesh has two sides. It is not only sinful; it is also good. When one thinks about sinful things, death comes to the soul even while it is still living. Covetous, materialistic desires; adulterous, lustful thoughts; stealing, lying, and the like all smother true life.

But this is not the fleshly problem referred to in Romans 8. The problem here is the good things of the flesh—that is, the keeping of a religious law (v. 3); in other words, trying to be good. In Romans 8, Paul was considering the fleshly effort to keep the Jewish law. Today, this law isn't our problem. However, your flesh may still be working hard to maintain your family's standards or those of your church, community, or ethnic group. Setting your mind on these things will inevitably make them a point of pride and exclusivity. Your effort to do good brings death to your soul while it is still living. So Paul says, "To set the mind on the flesh is death" (v. 6 NRSV).

In other words, to set the mind on the flesh is to eat of the tree of the knowledge of good and evil (Genesis 2:17). You do this and you die—not a physical death, but a spiritual one. You lose that inner ebullience and "bounce" that God freely gives to those who have faith. And you lose the ability to love (Matthew 22:37–40).

Keep in mind the story about the religious leader who asked Jesus, " 'Good teacher, what must I do to inherit eternal life?'

" 'Why do you call me good?' Jesus answered. 'No one is good—except God alone' " (Luke 18:18–19 NIV).

Since only God is good, let's follow the psalmist: Command our souls to bless the Lord, turn away from our fleshly self-effort, set our minds on the Spirit, love the Lord, and enjoy his Word. Then life and peace are ours (Romans 8:6).

59

REMEMBER
me, O LORD,
with the favour that thou
bearest unto thy people:
O visit me with thy salvation;
that I may see the good of thy chosen,
that I may rejoice in the gladness of thy nation,
that I may glory with thine inheritance.

PSALM 106:4–5

THINGS CHANGE; THIS IS OBVIOUS.

And even though Jesus Christ is the same yesterday and today and forever (Hebrews 13:8), unforeseen changes in spiritual life are inevitable and jarring. They dig deep into the heart. They expose what you cherish other than Christ.

Have you been as successful as Job with a good home life and church life? Have you been as strong as Samson with potent prayer and fellowship? Then maybe you've experienced the loss of these things as well and felt desolate and forgotten.

Job was the greatest of all the people of the east (Job 1:3). But he lost it all. So he prayed, "O that thou wouldest hide me in the grave, that thou wouldest keep me secret, until thy wrath be past." Job prayed like the psalmist, "That thou wouldest appoint me a set time, and remember me!" (14:13).

God did remember Job, and although his life turned out to be much the same as before, inwardly he was a changed man. He confessed, "Therefore I have uttered what I did not understand, things too wonderful for me, which I did not know. . . . I had heard of you by the hearing of the ear, but now my eye sees you" (Job 42:3, 5 NRSV).

Then there's the story of Samson. It's well-known. He took a Nazarite's vow of consecration to the Lord (Judges 13:7), the Spirit was upon him, and he was a mighty judge of Israel. But he lost his power (16:19) and was blinded and imprisoned by his enemies. Then Samson called to the Lord, "O Lord GOD, remember me, I pray thee, and strengthen me, I pray thee, only this once, O God, that I may be at once avenged of the Philistines for my two eyes" (v. 28). God answered his prayer, and Samson conquered more of his enemies at his death than he did in all his life (v. 30).

God remembers you as your life changes. This frees you to forget the past and look forward to what lies ahead, pressing toward the goal for the prize of the heavenly call of God in Christ Jesus (Philippians 3:13–14).

60

THEY

that go down to the sea in ships,
that do business in great waters;
these see the works of the LORD,
and his wonders in the deep.
For he commandeth,
and raiseth the stormy wind,
which lifteth up the waves thereof. . . .

Then they cry unto the LORD in their trouble,
and he bringeth them out of their distresses.
He maketh the storm a calm,
so that the waves thereof are still.
Then are they glad because they be quiet;
so he bringeth them unto their desired haven.

PSALM 107:23–25, 28–30

THE ENCYCLOPEDIA BRITANNICA SAYS,

"The casualties suffered by the participants in World War I dwarfed those of previous wars: some 8,500,000 soldiers died as a result of wounds and/or disease. The greatest number of casualties and wounds were inflicted by artillery, followed by small arms, and then by poison gas." Great Britain lost so many soldiers on the battlefields of France that the postwar streets of London were bereft of young men. Theirs was called "the lost generation."

But there is a story of a platoon of British soldiers in the trenches that suffered not one casualty. Every day, together they read and prayed Psalm 91: "Those who live in the shelter of the Most High will find rest in the shadow of the Almighty. . . . He alone is my refuge, my place of safety; he is my God, and I am trusting him. . . . He will shelter you with his feathers. His faithful promises are your armor and protection. Do not be afraid of the terrors of the night, nor fear the dangers of the day, nor dread the plague that stalks in darkness, nor the disaster that strikes at midday"

(Psalm 91:1–2, 4–6 NLT).

These soldiers found themselves in a perilous, impossible situation. In this, they weren't unlike the people in Psalm 107. Some wandered in "desert wastes" (v. 4 NRSV) and others were imprisoned "in darkness and in gloom" (v. 10 NRSV). "Some were sick through their sinful ways" (v. 17 NRSV) while others "went down to the sea in ships" (v. 23 NRSV). But they all cried to the Lord in their trouble and he delivered them from their distress (vv. 6, 13, 19, 28).

Psalm 91 promises, "Surely he shall deliver thee from the snare of the fowler, and from the noisome pestilence" (v. 3). Life may someday put you into the fire just as those soldiers were in the terror of the trenches. Maybe it already has. Maybe you are there right now being refined like silver, tested like gold. If so, remember Scripture's testimony: "They will call on my name, and I will answer them. I will say, 'They are my people'; and they will say, 'The LORD is our God'" (Zechariah 13:9 NRSV).

61

O God,

my heart is fixed;
I will sing and give praise, even with my glory.
Awake, psaltery and harp:
I myself will awake early.
I will praise thee, O Lord, among the people:
and I will sing praises unto
thee among the nations.
For thy mercy is great above the heavens:
and thy truth reacheth unto the clouds.

Psalm 108:1–4

JUST
AS WE AWAKEN
EVERY MORNING TO

live our day-to-day life, so it is with a spiritual life. Like striking a chord on the strings of a harp, the psalmist wakes himself up to praise the Lord. David sang almost the same song in Psalm 57:8–10. It must have been a habit for him. His heart was fixed, centered like the hub of a wheel.

John Wells wrote about the habit of prayer and meditation on God: "As we know, a garden which is watered with sudden showers is more uncertain in its fruit than when it is refreshed with a constant stream; so when our thoughts are sometimes on good things, and then run off; when they only take a glance of a holy object, and then flit away, there is not so much fruit brought into the soul" (from the *Practical Sabbatarian*, 1668). In prayer, you water your heart with the object of your prayer—that is, God.

Or you may think of your prayer like tea steeping in water—soon the water changes into tea. Similarly, as you spend time in prayer, your heart steeps in the Holy Spirit of God until, like David, you say, "O God, my heart is fixed."

Remember how Mary "kept all these things, and pondered them in her heart" (Luke 2:19)? This is meditative prayer—fixing the mind on godly things; staking them down like a tent upon the ground of Christ. Just as when the disciples saw Christ in transfiguration: Could they take their eyes off of him? No. They said, "It is good for us to be here" (Matthew 17:1–4). Their hearts were fixed.

62

I LOVE

the LORD, because he hath heard my voice
and my supplications.
Because he hath inclined his ear unto me,
therefore will I call upon him as long as I live.

PSALM 116:1–2

THESE
WOULD BE
SUCH PLEASANT WORDS

if the next verse weren't so grim. Imagine—
what in your life would cause you to say, "The
sorrows of death compassed me, and the pains
of hell gat hold upon me: I found trouble and
sorrow" (v. 3)?

These words invoke the image of hunters
and dogs surrounding their prey. No way of escape is left for David. He is enclosed in a ring of
deadly grief. So the pains of hell caught hold of
him like the teeth of the hunting hounds. Death
and hell had found him, and he in turn found
trouble and sorrow. Trouble on the outside, sorrow within.

If you had asked David, "How are you?" he
would never have casually replied, "I'm fine;
how are you?" In no way did he lessen his dangers and tribulations. He never concealed his
soul's distress. Instead David clearly and willingly described it. Why? In this way, Israel's
king gave God glory and reduced himself to a
supplicant for God's help.

Likewise, the apostle Paul often told of his
troubles, foibles, and weaknesses. Both the

king and the apostle show that Christians do God a disservice when they put on a happy face, when they "let a smile be their umbrella."

After all, Paul said, "Most gladly therefore will I rather glory in my infirmities, that the power of Christ may rest upon me. Therefore I take pleasure in infirmities, in reproaches, in necessities, in persecutions, in distresses for Christ's sake: for when I am weak, then am I strong" (2 Corinthians 12:9–10).

But please note: One must also follow David's way of prayer: "Then called I upon the name of the LORD; O LORD, I beseech thee, deliver my soul" (Psalm 116:4). Then your testimony can also be the same as his: "I love the LORD, because he hath heard my voice and my supplications. Because he hath inclined his ear unto me, therefore will I call upon him as long as I live" (vv. 1–2).

63

O GIVE

thanks unto the LORD; for he is good:
because his mercy endureth for ever.
Let Israel now say,
that his mercy endureth for ever.
Let the house of Aaron now say,
that his mercy endureth for ever.
Let them now that fear the LORD say,
that his mercy endureth for ever.

PSALM 118:1–4

THE
PHARISEES
WERE THE LEADING

sect in first-century Judaism, a small but influential group of about six thousand men. Today we would call them a lay fellowship. Committed to strict observance of all the traditional ordinances, they painstakingly carried out religious duties such as tithing and ceremonial washing.

The chief concern of the Pharisees was accurate interpretation of Scripture. But this had created strife over the proper maintenance of the traditions of Judaism. As a result, the Pharisees were out of touch with ordinary Israelites who were not concerned with such things. The Gospels graphically describe the pharisaic attitude of contempt for the great majority of Jews who lacked knowledge of the law and intense commitment to the traditions (John 7:47–49).

But the Pharisees were entirely unlike the God they professed to follow. While God's mercy endures forever, they were merciless. This is why Jesus warned them, "Woe unto you, scribes and Pharisees, hypocrites! for ye pay tithe of mint and anise and cummin, and have omitted the weightier matters of the law, judgment, mercy, and faith: these ought ye to have done" (Matthew 23:23).

Jesus challenged the Pharisees' fundamental outlook on life: "You strain at a gnat," he said, "but swallow a camel" (see v. 24). In other words, "Holiness is not found in your careful religious observances. You are preoccupied with details like the tithing of herbs, yet you have completely missed the true message of the law and the prophets."

Those ancient Pharisees are long gone. But the same trap to which they fell victim still waits to snare good Christians. The way to safely spring that snare is to understand the true message of the law and the prophets. This message is condensed in Micah 6:6–8 (NRSV):

> *With what shall I come before the LORD,*
> *and bow myself before God on high?*
> *Shall I come before him with burnt offer-*
> *ings, with calves a year old? Will the*
> *LORD be pleased with thousands of rams,*
> *with ten thousands of rivers of oil? . . .*
> *He has told you, O mortal, what is good;*
> *and what does the LORD require of you*
> *but to do justice, and to love kindness,*
> *and to walk humbly with your God?*

64

I CALLED

upon the LORD in distress:
the LORD answered me,
and set me in a large place.

PSALM 118:5

I ONCE LIVED WITH MY WIFE AND

children in a cottage by the beach. It was built all by hand, of stone outside and wood paneling within—it looked like a storybook house. When the morning fog from the Long Island Sound lifted, sunshine poured in a particular window and washed across the daybed. This marked the spot that our marvelous Abyssinian cat, Samson, claimed as his own.

It wasn't only the sunshine that made the daybed a perfect place for Samson the cat. From that position he had long clear views of the first floor of the cottage. This gave him a powerful position. He was safe because he could see so far through the house. He could also hunt from there because he could see anything that moved—usually houseflies.

When the psalmist called on the Lord, the Lord's answer was to set him in a large place—a place like my cat's daybed. The psalmist found himself in a safe, broad place like a large meadow or plain. He was given a clear view of what was around him; he could see his position in the larger scheme of things.

Calm, careful, prayerful reading and study of the Bible will usher you to a position in a broad place. It reveals the gospel, opening your eyes to what is really around you. It turns you from darkness to light and from the power of Satan to God, so you may receive forgiveness of sins and a place among those who are sanctified by faith in Jesus Christ (see Acts 26:18). Contrariwise, without the Scripture, our hearts grow dull and our spiritual ears hard of hearing.

Are you ever distressed, like the psalmist? Here is what this is like: " 'They have shut their eyes; so that they might not look with their eyes, and listen with their ears, and understand with their heart and turn—and I would heal them' " (Acts 28:27 NRSV).

This is the distress out from which we must call on the Lord. Then the Lord answers by setting us in a large place.

65

Deal

bountifully with thy servant,
that I may live, and keep thy word.
Open thou mine eyes,
that I may behold wondrous things
out of thy law.
I am a stranger in the earth:
hide not thy commandments from me.
My soul breaketh for the longing that it hath
unto thy judgments at all times.

Psalm 119:17–20

No one can know the things of the

Scriptures unless Christ opens his eyes, so the psalmist prays, "Open thou mine eyes" (v. 18). He was like Bartimaeus the blind man who knew one simple fact: He could not follow Jesus unless he could see him.

Jesus once asked Bartimaeus, "What do you want me to do for you?"

" 'Teacher,' the blind man said, 'I want to see!'

"And Jesus said to him, 'Go your way. Your faith has healed you.' And instantly the blind man could see! Then he followed Jesus down the road" (Mark 10:51–52 NLT).

Notice that the psalmist doesn't complain that the law is hard to understand. He doesn't pray, "Lord, make your law more intelligible." Rather, he knows that he himself cannot understand the law unless God opens his eyes to its meaning. After all, a blind man doesn't complain that there is no light in the sun. He knows it's there. The problem is that the blind man can't see it.

There is no lack of spiritual light in the

Scripture—it is the "light that shines in a dark place" (2 Peter 1:19 NKJV). But there can be a veil of darkness upon our hearts when we read it (2 Corinthians 3:14). If we cannot see the Scripture's clear light, the defect is not in the Scripture, but in ourselves.

Here is a prayer that you might wish to pray. It will help heal this defect:

God of my LORD Jesus Christ, the Father of glory, give me a spirit of wisdom and revelation in the knowledge of yourself. Enlighten the eyes of my understanding that I may know what is the hope of my calling, and what are the riches of the glory of your inheritance in the saints, and what is the exceeding greatness of your power to us who believe. Do this, I pray, according to the working of your mighty power, which you put in Christ when you raised him from the dead, and set him at your own right hand in the heavenly places.

EPHESIANS 1:17–20,

AUTHOR'S PARAPHRASE

66

I CRIED

with my whole heart;
hear me, O LORD: I will keep thy statutes.
I cried unto thee;
save me, and I shall keep thy testimonies.
I prevented the dawning of
the morning, and cried:
I hoped in thy word.
Mine eyes prevent the night watches,
that I might meditate in thy word.

PSALM 119:145–148

THE PSALMIST WHOLEHEARTEDLY CRIED OUT TO GOD.

Don't you wonder, "What is a whole heart?" Maybe the obverse of a whole heart is a partial heart. If so, what is missing from one's heart if it is partial?

Once God promised, "I will give them an heart to know me, that I am the LORD: and they shall be my people, and I will be their God: for they shall return unto me with their whole heart" (Jeremiah 24:7). And God did as promised, giving a new covenant in which the law is no longer written on stone tablets but on the human heart (31:33; Hebrews 8:10). In this new covenant, the law is not applied to a people cosmetically but is lived by them organically.

This was worked out practically when Jesus Christ came not to abolish the law but to fulfill it (Matthew 5:17). When this man, who was the fulfillment of the law, died and was resurrected, it became possible for the human heart to become whole. God is now able to strengthen men and women with power by his Spirit in their inner beings so that Christ can dwell in their hearts by faith (Ephesians 3:16–17).

With Christ dwelling in your heart, it is no longer partial. It is whole. And then, with others, you can become rooted and grounded in God's love. You can begin to comprehend what is the breadth, and length, and depth, and height of that love, and eventually be filled with all the fullness of God (vv. 18–19).

Not only so, but you can pray to God with a whole heart, a Christ-filled heart.

67

I WILL

lift up mine eyes unto the hills,
from whence cometh my help.
My help cometh from the LORD,
which made heaven and earth.

PSALM 121:1–2

THE
FIRST HILL
FROM WHICH HELP

came to Israel was the mountain named Sinai. "There the angel of the LORD appeared to [Moses] in a flame of fire out of a bush; he looked, and the bush was blazing, yet it was not consumed. Then Moses said, 'I must turn aside and look at this great sight, and see why the bush is not burned up'" (Exodus 3:2–3 NRSV). The New Testament calls this "the story about the bush" (Mark 12:26 and Luke 20:37 NRSV; see also Acts 7:35), not the story about the flame, or even about the burning bush. Help came to Israel out of a no-name, generic thorn-bush growing on a remote mountainside.

Moses mentioned this bush in his final words when blessing the tribe of Joseph "with the choice gifts of the earth and its fullness, and the favor of the one who dwells in the bush" (Deuteronomy 33:16 NRSV, see translation footnote). How significant. Moses' last remembrance of God is of the one who dwells in the bush! He had met with God numerous times on Mount Sinai and in the tabernacle. But at the end of his life, Moses recollects his first divine encounter—the story of the bush.

The New Testament begins with a similar divine encounter. But here God comes not in a thornbush but as an ordinary man—Jesus. The prophet Isaiah described him like this: "He had no form or majesty that we should look at him, nothing in his appearance that we should desire him. He was despised and rejected by others; a man of suffering and acquainted with infirmity; and as one who hides his face from us he was despised, and we held him of no account" (53:2–3 NRSV, see translation footnote).

For us, the story of the bush is the gospel of God incarnate. God came down from the heavenly mountain to help us. God lived as a thorny, unattractive man named Jesus. Today those people who, like Moses, turn aside for a closer look, see the man in whom all the fullness of the Godhead was pleased to dwell (Colossians 1:19): Jesus Christ, the unforgettable thornbush—blazing yet not consumed.

68

LORD,

hear my voice:
let thine ears be attentive to
the voice of my supplications.
If thou, LORD, shouldest mark iniquities,
O Lord, who shall stand?
But there is forgiveness with thee,
that thou mayest be feared.
I wait for the LORD, my soul doth wait,
and in his word do I hope.
My soul waiteth for the LORD
more than they that watch for the morning:
I say, more than they that
watch for the morning.

PSALM 130:2–6

YOUR
LIFE AS A
CHRISTIAN RELIES

entirely on who God is—not at all on what
you are. This is why the Christian faith has
such power. And this is why the ancient poet
wrote, "My soul waiteth for the Lord more
than they that watch for the morning." The
poet's soul was intensely focused on God, not
on himself.

A Scottish hymn-writer named Horatius
Bonar (1808–1889) said it this way:

> *Not what I am, O Lord,*
> *but what thou art;*
> *That alone can be my soul's true rest;*
> *Thy love, not mine, bids fear*
> *and doubt depart,*
> *And stills the tempest of my tossing breast.*

The first letter of John explains how this
can be: "We have seen and testify that the
Father has sent his Son to be the Savior of the
world. If anyone acknowledges that Jesus is
the Son of God, God lives in him and he in
God. And so we know and rely on the love

God has for us" (1 John 4:14–16 NIV). John is so clear, so concise.

Long before John, the ancient psalmist seems to have understood the gospel. So he could pray, "If thou, LORD, shouldest mark iniquities, O Lord, who shall stand? But there is forgiveness with thee." In other words, if God were to punish you for the things you do, you'd be dead right now. What's worse, Christ's death would be meaningless. But "God showed his great love for us by sending Christ to die for us *while we were still sinners*." (Romans 5:8 NLT, italics supplied). And we are still sinners to this day. Horatius Bonar made this truth his poem:

> *'Tis what I know of thee, my Lord and God,*
> *That fills my soul with peace,*
> > *my lips with song;*
> *Thou art my hearth, my joy, my staff, my rod;*
> *Leaning on thee, in weakness I am strong.*
>
> *More of thyself, oh, show me, hour by hour;*
> *More of thy glory, O my God and Lord;*
> *More of thyself in all thy grace and power;*
> *More of thy love and truth, incarnate Word.*

69

LORD,

my heart is not haughty, nor mine eyes lofty:
neither do I exercise myself in great matters,
or in things too high for me.
Surely I have behaved and quieted myself,
as a child that is weaned of his mother:
my soul is even as a weaned child.

PSALM 131:1–2

SOME
PEOPLE SAY
THAT THAT PSALM 131

is a song the Israelites sang when returning from their Babylonian captivity. Their hearts were humble and weaned from idols—objects that had enthralled and removed them from the love of God. Today our idols are not carved images as they were in those days. But we do still have to contend with the very first idol—the knowledge of good and evil, right versus wrong, us against them (Genesis 2:17). This is the most potent of all golden calves.

Because of this idol, Paul wrote about his jealousy for the believers. "I am jealous for you with the jealousy of God himself. I promised you as a pure bride to one husband, Christ," he declared (2 Corinthians 11:2 NLT). But he feared that, just as Eve was deceived by the serpent to eat the tree of the knowledge of good and evil, somehow the church would be led away from pure and simple devotion to Christ (v. 3).

The apostle told the church in Corinth, "You seem to believe whatever anyone tells you, even if they preach about a different Jesus than the one we preach, or a different Spirit than the one you received, or a different kind of gospel than the one you believed" (v. 4 NLT). These deceptions have their source among men who exercise themselves in things too high for them. So they fall into the idolatrous morass of the knowledge of good and evil.

Some people throughout church history have exercised themselves in great matters yet had the humility to avoid idolatry. Anselm of Canterbury (1033–1109), the outstanding Christian philosopher and theologian of the eleventh century, was one. Perhaps you can make Anselm's prayer your own:

> *I do not seek, O Lord, to penetrate thy depths. I by no means think my intellect equal to them; but I long to understand in some degree thy truth, which my heart believes and loves. For I do not seek to understand that I may believe; but I believe, that I may understand.*

70

O LORD,

thou hast searched me, and known me.
Thou knowest my downsitting
and mine uprising,
thou understandest my thought afar off.
Thou compassest my path and my lying down,
and art acquainted with all my ways.
For there is not a word in my tongue,
but, lo, O LORD, thou knowest it altogether.

PSALM 139:1–4

CHRISTIANS ARE ACCUSTOMED TO THE IDEA THAT GOD

made the sun and sky, the "moon and stars, which [he has] ordained." We don't doubt the fact that they are "the work of [God's] fingers" (Psalm 8:3). But we go much further than this if we admit to the Lord, "you know when I sit down and when I stand up" (see 139:2).

This fact is mentioned several times in Scripture as though it were very important. It seems that even eternity hinges on these words: "The LORD shall preserve thy going out and thy coming in from this time forth, and even for evermore" (Psalm 121:8).

In such little matters as sitting down and standing up, does God watch over you? It is incomprehensible that not an action is lost or a thought overlooked by God. No wonder that as David relates these tiny miracles of care he suddenly declares, "Such knowledge is too wonderful for me; it is high, I cannot attain unto it" (139:6).

Yet it is true, and the New Testament teaches the same: "Neither is there any creature that is not manifest in his sight: but all things are naked and opened unto the eyes of him with whom we have to do" (Hebrews 4:13). Even in Revelation, the most cryptic book of Scripture, seven times Christ clearly says, "I know thy works" (2:2, 9, 13, 19; 3:1, 8, 15).

This is clear: We can never escape from the Spirit or get away from God's presence. Can you go to heaven? God is there. How about in the place of the dead? There too. Catch a ride on the morning wind to camp on the remotest beach; even there the divine hand guides you and almighty strength supports you (Psalm 139:7–10).

This is true: We live and move and have our being in the one who is above all and through all and in all (Acts 17:28; Ephesians 4:6).

71

FOR

thou hast possessed my reins:
thou hast covered me in my mother's womb.
I will praise thee; for I am fearfully
and wonderfully made:
marvellous are thy works;
and that my soul knoweth right well.
My substance was not hid from thee,
when I was made in secret,
and curiously wrought in the
lowest parts of the earth.
Thine eyes did see my substance,
yet being unperfect;
and in thy book all my members were written,
which in continuance were fashioned,
when as yet there was none of them.

PSALM 139:13–16

"THE LORD GOD FORMED MAN FROM

the dust of the ground, and breathed into his nostrils the breath of life; and the man became a living being" (Genesis 2:7 NRSV). What did God do after this? Stop making man? Did God make the first man, and ever since that time have we been making one another through procreation? No. As Job said, "God created both me and my servants. He created us both" (Job 31:15 NLT).

David agrees: "I am fearfully and wonderfully made: marvellous are thy works" (Psalm 139:14). Meaning: "Lord, I am distinctively made, and you have made me." David didn't give credit for his existence to his father or mother. He was made by God as much as Adam was.

One day Esau asked his brother Jacob, "Who are those with thee?" Jacob replied, "The children which God hath graciously given thy servant" (Genesis 33:5). Certainly, we are begotten and born of earthly parents, yet God, the chief parent, is our only maker. So Paul bowed his knees to the "Father of our

Lord Jesus Christ, of whom the whole family in heaven and earth is named" (Ephesians 3:14–15).

We "know that the LORD is God. It is he that made us, and we are his; we are his people, and the sheep of his pasture." (Psalm 100:3 NRSV). So take confidence to pray with the apostle that the maker of your entire being would "sanctify you wholly; . . .your whole spirit and soul and body be preserved blameless unto the coming of our Lord Jesus Christ" (1 Thessalonians 5:23).

72

DELIVER

me, O LORD, from the evil man:
preserve me from the violent man;
which imagine mischiefs in their heart;
continually are they gathered together for war.
They have sharpened their tongues
like a serpent; adders' poison is under their lips.

PSALM 140:1–3

THE
READER OF
THIS PSALM MIGHT

think that it is fierce and bitter. David utters words in prayer that we might not even say in anger. He tells God that his enemies are evil and violent with mischief in their heart, serpents' tongues, and mouths full of poison. David calls curses upon them. "Let burning coals fall upon them: let them be cast into the fire; into deep pits, that they rise not up again. Let not an evil speaker be established in the earth: evil shall hunt the violent man to overthrow him" (Psalm 140:10–11).

Are these curses consistent with the character of a child of God? Are they becoming of David, the king anointed by God? Yet can you find fault with someone who prays out his pain to God? David was smarting under injury and wrong and simply laid open his heart to God. King or pauper, you can't go wrong if you honestly tell God what you think and feel. Some people call this *confession*.

Your prayer may begin like David's, with an unkindly spirit. The apostle Paul once echoed the attitude of David's prayer: "Their throat is an open sepulchre," he wrote in Romans. "With their tongues they have used deceit; the poison of asps is under their lips" (3:13).

I know a woman who occasionally turns to prayer with such anger that she actually curses at God. What does such honest prayer do for her? It eventually reveals her own guiltiness. It gives her a sight of her own wrongs towards God. So she is humbled, healed, and soothed.

Kneel to pray out your troubles to God just as David did. When you do, you'll remember you are a child of your Father in heaven who makes his sun rise on the evil and on the good, and sends rain on the just and on the unjust (Matthew 5:45). May this open your heart to pray for all such people.

73

I LOOKED

on my right hand, and beheld,
but there was no man that would know me:
refuge failed me; no man cared for my soul.
I cried unto thee, O LORD: I said,
Thou art my refuge and my
portion in the land of the living.
Attend unto my cry;
for I am brought very low:
deliver me from my persecutors;
for they are stronger than I.

PSALM 142:4–6

ONE
DAY THE
PROPHET ELIJAH

prophesied to King Ahab of an approaching drought. This displeased the king greatly. Suddenly Elijah was like the psalmist who cried, "I looked on my right hand, and beheld, but there was no man that would know me: refuge failed me; no man cared for my soul" (Psalm 142:4). So God told him to flee to the Cherith Ravine east of the Jordan River. There Elijah was miraculously fed by ravens and drank the water of the wadi. Soon the drought he predicted arrived (1 Kings 17:1–7).

Not long after, Elijah challenged Ahab's pagan priests to a contest to see whose god would accept their sacrifice. Of course Elijah won the contest. He prayed only once and "immediately the fire of the LORD flashed down from heaven and burned up the young bull." Then Elijah proceeded to kill all the 850 prophets of Baal and Asherah! (18:22–40 NLT).

Then he ran for his life! He was courageous when he stood by his sacrifice and the fire of God fell upon it and when he killed every one of those godless prophets. But Elijah's courage and trust in God failed, so he ran for his life and hid in the ravine (19:3). Only this time God had not told him to retreat. So no ravens were waiting to feed him and the wadi was dry.

Elijah "sat down under a solitary broom tree" in the ravine (v. 4 NLT). While doing God's work back in Israel, he depended upon God's protection. But when he fled, Elijah found that his only protection from the cruel desert were the leaves of a scrawny broom tree.

Burning there in the partial shade, Elijah said, "I have had enough, LORD. Take my life." But first he confessed his sin: "I am no better than my ancestors" (v. 4 NLT). He recognized that he was no improvement on those Israelites who in this very wilderness under the same burning sun had rebelled against God and wandered their own way for forty years. Then Elijah lay down to die in his sleep. Yet he awoke as angels, not ravens, provided him with food and drink. His confession evoked God's forgiveness. God brought Elijah back to the land of the living and again became his safety and refuge.

74

CAUSE

*me to hear thy lovingkindness
in the morning;
for in thee do I trust:
cause me to know the way
wherein I should walk;
for I lift up my soul unto thee.
Deliver me, O LORD, from mine enemies:
I flee unto thee to hide me.*

PSALM 143:8–9

THESE ARE THREE PRAYERS THAT A

believer may use each day: at night, in the morning, and at day's end.

Although Christ advised that you "take no thought for tomorrow" (see Matthew 6:34), it is wise to begin a day the night before by praying, "Cause me to hear thy lovingkindness in the morning; for in thee do I trust" (Psalm 143:8). When making this request, you are not worrying, "What will I eat and drink? What will I wear?" (see Matthew 6:31). There is but one valid concern for tomorrow—that your heart would be attuned to God's love when you first awake.

God will answer the night's prayer and enable you to rise in the morning with fresh trust and strength to pray, "Cause me to know the way wherein I should walk; for I lift up my soul unto thee" (Psalm 143:8). This is a prayer for God's guidance in the day's affairs. Yet God can use your help in this task—as you pass through the day, lift your soul to him.

To lift the soul can mean many things that are unique to you, just as your day belongs to you alone. Will you lift your soul above gossip? Will you lift it above aggressive driving? Stealing time or pilfering pencils at the office? Harboring resentment? Exchanging words with your spouse? Criticizing others? If your soul will not rise of itself, lift it yourself—lift it to God.

As the sun sets, failures, disappointments, and fears can arise. These are your enemies. So the day's final prayer is for Christ's cleansing, forgiveness, and preservation: "Deliver me, O LORD, from mine enemies: I flee unto thee to hide me" (v. 9).

And so, when the sufficient evil of the day has passed (Matthew 6:34), God listens for you to pray once more, "Cause me to hear thy lovingkindness in the morning; for in thee do I trust."

75

PRAISE

the LORD from the earth,
ye dragons, and all deeps:
fire, and hail; snow, and vapours;
stormy wind fulfilling his word:
mountains, and all hills;
fruitful trees, and all cedars:
beasts, and all cattle;
creeping things, and flying fowl:
kings of the earth, and all people;
princes, and all judges of the earth:
both young men, and maidens;
old men, and children.

PSALM 148:7–12

SIMPLE FAITH TELLS US THAT RAIN COMES

from God. But people scoff at this idea. After all, science has discovered that precipitation is the product of certain physical laws of air, water, and heat. No matter, the faithful are enlightened to see who is the real actor in the meteorological drama. Mark Twain famously said, "Everybody talks about the weather but nobody does anything about it." If weather were a matter of simple physics, somebody could do something about it.

Suppose a friend sends you a gift of beautiful workmanship. But as you respond with gratitude, someone tries to lessen the beauty of the gift and the honor of the giver by telling you that it is the product of machinery in a nearby factory. He does not see that the real beauty of the gift, and its source is the giver's heart of love. It is God who sends rain in love on the righteous and the unrighteous alike (Matthew 5:45). The principles of physics are the secondary cause of rain. God "established the force of the wind and measured out the waters, when he made a decree for the rain and a path for the thunderstorm, then he looked at wisdom and appraised it; he confirmed it and tested it" (Job 28:25–27 NIV).

The psalmist calls to the hail, snow, and vapors to bear a part in the work of praise to God. Not that they are able to do this actively. Rather, we are to enlist the assistance of the whole creation in honoring God. We do this by caring for all creatures and their earthly homes. Secondly, we receive what is offered by the creation with thanksgiving to God. And, finally, with affection, we offer back to God what we receive from God's creation.

Snow and hail and other created things cannot actually bless and praise God, but they serve us well so that we can bless the God of love for all the gifts of creation.

Inspirational Library

Beautiful purse/pocket-size editions of Christian classics bound in flexible leatherette. These books make thoughtful gifts for everyone on your list, including yourself!

When I'm on My Knees   The highly popular collection of devotional thoughts on prayer, especially for women.
  Flexible Leatherette $4.97

The Bible Promise Book   Over 1,000 promises from God's Word arranged by topic. What does God promise about matters like: Anger, Illness, Jealousy, Love, Money, Old Age, and Mercy? Find out in this book!
  Flexible Leatherette $3.97

Daily Wisdom for Women   A daily devotional for women seeking biblical wisdom to apply to their lives. Scripture taken from the New American Standard Version of the Bible.
  Flexible Leatherette $4.97

My Daily Prayer Journal   Each page is dated and features a Scripture verse and ample room for you to record your thoughts, prayers, and praises. One page for each day of the year.
  Flexible Leatherette $4.97

Available wherever books are sold.
Or order from:

Barbour Publishing, Inc.
P.O. Box 719
Uhrichsville, OH 44683
http://www.barbourbooks.com

If you order by mail, add $2.00 to your order for shipping.
Prices are subject to change without notice.